Praise for
Waves of Healing

"*Waves of Healing* is a powerful and inspirational book—a must-read for anyone with a loved one on the autism spectrum. You will laugh and you will cry as author Cash Lambert passionately shares both the struggles and the triumphs of the autism journey as sand and surf become a form of therapy and healing for so many families."

—Amy KD Tobik, editor-in chief of *Autism Parenting Magazine*

"Surfers and water-lovers have long talked about the mysterious healing power of the sea. With empathy, attention to detail, and skillful story-telling, Cash Lambert shows how real that healing power is, taking us deep into the struggles of living with autism, deep into the joyful stories of children literally paddling and riding their way to greater health and happiness. This is such a hopeful and potentially life-changing read."

—Jaimal Yogis, author of *All Our Waves Are Water* and *Saltwater Buddha*

"*Waves of Healing* is a big-hearted story that will delight anyone who loves the ocean. Saltwater is a universal balm—Cash Lambert knows this deeply, and his commitment to sharing his experience in the surf with autistic kids and their families makes for an inspiring tale, beautifully told."

—Susan Casey, author of *Voices in the Ocean: A Journey Into the Wild and Haunting World of Dolphins*

"*Waves of Healing* shows how a creative, nature-based approach is often the best way for healing and hope to flow into the lives of those coping with autism and into all lives. Lambert has written a book that is both important and profound."

—David Athey, Professor of English, Palm Beach Atlantic University, author of *Joan of the Everglades*

"As a firm believer in the many blessings of surf therapy for children on the spectrum, I was delighted to read Cash Lambert's uplifting and validating account of a season on the shore with Surfers for Autism. He writes with the head and heart of a surfer about the thrilling transformation that finds many children and families on the back of their shared surfing experiences—a must-read for anyone who accepts the healing power of stoke, and the rich, restorative energy to be mined from a community of like-minded souls.
—Daniel Paisner, co-author of *Scratching the Horizon: A Surfing Life*

"Perfect waves and empty beaches, the sport of surfing is easily romanticized, but at its core it possesses the power to change one's life. For those who struggle with autism, surfing can mean a freedom and joy like they've never experienced. Author Cash Lambert has taken the time to tell the story of this unlikely relationship. He tenderly makes the case for the healing powers of the sea, as well as how and why it can be so therapeutic for those on the autism spectrum. *Waves of Healing* will stoke you out, it will tug on your heartstrings, and it will make you reconsider what those with autism are capable of—and how one good ride can change everything."
—Jake Howard, surf writer and editor of *First Priority: A Father's Journey in Raising World Champion Surfer Carissa Moore*

"Often, it's difficult to understand the everyday struggles and small milestones that families raising a child with autism face, but Cash Lambert's firsthand ride-along—both on land and in the sea—truly puts their lives into perspective. A deeply honest and eloquent account, *Waves of Healing* is a story of hope, and a discovery of what the therapeutic power of the ocean—and organizations like Surfers For Autism—can do."
—Beau Flemister, former editor-at-large of Surfing Magazine and author of *In the Seat of a Stranger's Car*

Waves of Healing

HOW SURFING CHANGES
THE LIVES OF CHILDREN
WITH AUTISM

Cash Lambert

Hatherleigh Press is committed to preserving and protecting the natural resources of the earth. Environmentally responsible and sustainable practices are embraced within the company's mission statement.

Visit us at www.hatherleighpress.com and register online for free offers, discounts, special events, and more.

WAVES OF HEALING

Library of Congress Cataloging-in-Publication Data is available upon request.
ISBN: 978-1-57826-794-1

Cover and Interior Design by Carolyn Kasper
Cover photography by Ben Hicks (benjhicks.com)

Printed in the United States
10 9 8 7 6 5 4 3 2 1

CONTENTS

To all those who have surfed for autism:
this is your story.

INTRODUCTION

Have you ever been told that something could change your life?

Maybe it was an investment, a "sure thing." Maybe it was a magic pill, a career change—even a piece of cutting-edge technology.

Maybe you gave it a shot, maybe you didn't. But odds are, it didn't really change your life. So, like a balloon deflating, your budding hopes and desires disappeared. Skepticism set in. "That only happens in Hollywood movies" became your mentality.

That's because opportunities that create true life change—where new passions are instilled that significantly change your life's trajectory—are few and far between.

And that's why, when they *do* show up, the moments they create are so special.

It's even more special for families of children with autism—a condition that sees children struggle against difficulties with social skills, repetitive behaviors and communication. A condition that affects one out of every 57 children in North America. A condition that irrevocably changes their lives, and the lives of everyone around them.

From the moment a diagnosis is reached, parents begin frantically searching for ways to help their child, leaving no stone unturned. Some are united by the challenge; others separate when the physical, emotional, and financial toll becomes too great.

Then, once a sense of behavioral stability is finally reached, parents continue to search for education and activities to help their child progress further. It's challenging. It's grueling. And it's a never-ending process.

That's why, when the opportunity for a true life change presented itself to families experiencing autism in Florida in 2008, it really was something special.

A new organization, Surfers for Autism, was promising to help autistic children in a new and unique way: through surfing. Many families were understandably hesitant; meltdowns, outbursts and pathological fear were very real risks when placing someone with autism onto a surfboard in the ocean.

But despite misgivings, on a Saturday morning in April of 2008, a group of surfers gathered on a South Florida beach to take children and teenagers with autism and other disabilities surfing.

No one at the event could have predicted what would come next. Throughout that day, 40 participants rode the waves into shore with smiles spread wide across their faces. Some, previously diagnosed as "nonverbal," cheered and raised their hands at their accomplishment as they neared the shoreline. Those not receptive to touch were holding hands with the volunteer surf instructors as they waded into the sea. Participants experienced calming effects; others appeared more focused, more attentive.

That day served not only as first event for the nonprofit organization Surfers for Autism—it was also the genesis of a community, one united by surfing and autism, that still thrives today. After that inaugural event, Surfers for Autism and its groupie-like community increased in size and influence. A "Surf Tour" was created that visits 10–13 cities and beach towns up and down Florida's golden sand coast throughout the year. Participant lists grew from 40 to 200. The volunteer sign-up list swelled.

My involvement with this eclectic community began as a volunteer surf instructor. The events featured live concerts, food trucks, and a chance to teach participants how to surf while spending time with other like-minded surf volunteers. In other words, these events were simply the place to be on the weekend.

But in the process, I got to see so many incredible moments and hear even more incredible stories—stories of overcoming odds, of breaking down barriers, of true life change. Stories that deserved to be told in Hollywood.

I was studying journalism in college at the time, and so I decided to put what I was learning in class into action. I wanted to try to tell a few of these stories.

Bylines with publications like *Eastern Surf Magazine, Autism Parenting Magazine* and *The Atlantic Current* soon followed. And as I met and interviewed families, I began hearing about life changes occurring on an even deeper level than I could have imagined.

Participants were experiencing "therapeutic benefits" thanks to surfing. Surfing had become—literally—a form of therapy, no co-pay required. Participants were finding their identities through the sport—some even developing a desire to compete.

Surfing had become an integral part of the participants' lives. Volunteers were developing a passion for helping those with disabilities, and many were pursuing a career in the industry. Mothers were in tears, fathers proudly cheered. Families met one another, and for the first time, found people with whom they could relate and vent. Bonds, born from saltwater and surfboards, were instantly created. The same went for siblings; for the first time, they could relate to someone else who had a sibling with autism.

What's more, a select group of families each had such a profound experience with surfing that they attended all or nearly all events during each Surf Tour—earning themselves the nickname "frequent fliers" and forming a tight-knit group of individuals who had fully embraced the healing power of surfing in their children's lives.

The surf therapy, the community, the camaraderie, the volunteering, the road trips, the early morning wake up calls, the wipeouts—these families were all in. It was only a matter of time before I was, too.

Through surfing, these inspiring families experienced, and continue to experience, healing and hope.

This is their story.

1

BREAKTHROUGHS

"The doctor said he was moderately mentally retarded and uneducable...He said it would get worse, too. That was the first anxiety attack I ever had."

Suddenly, the tone of Miranda Fuentes' voice seemed completely different.

She wanted little Andres to stand up on the surfboard, after she'd pushed it into a crashing wave. And for the past 15 minutes, she had been encouraging him in this course of action, hoping (and perhaps even praying) for it.

She knew that asking a child to stand on an unstable piece of foam floating in the turbulent Atlantic Ocean is hard enough—even when autism *isn't* involved.

"Up, Up, Up, Andres!" Like a religious chant, 17-year-old Miranda had been yelling this throughout the entire 15-minute surf session, struggling to have her plea heard above the roar of the crowded beach, the crashing of the waves, and the reggae music pumping out of the loudspeakers.

Miranda knew this task wasn't impossible for the 5-year-old; they'd practiced it on the beach together prior to the session. On the sand, he'd popped up into the surfing stance flawlessly—one foot forward, one foot back, hands spread parallel to the board.

She wanted him to stand on the surfboard because she knew about his diagnosis—Asperger's—and all the evaluations, the social delays, frustrations, and barriers that came with it. She wanted him to face his fears and progress; not only for her, but also for his parents, who stood on the beach with their camera, waiting for that magical moment.

But more than anything, she wanted Andres to stand for himself, so that he could feel the accomplishment of surfing a wave. An accomplishment that could then become his triumph, and no one else's.

Yet throughout the full heat, Andres opted instead for comfortable belly rides to shore. So it was that when the horn sounded, signifying the fifteenth minute was up, Miranda (knowing this was the last wave in the timed session) strode forward, pushed Andres into a wave, and let loose in a forceful tone: "Andres! Stand *up*! Up, Up, UP!"

There are few phrases in the English language that have an effect like, "Up, Up, Up," according to the lead beach marshal, Monica Valdes (Miranda's aunt), who led Surfers for Autism's first volunteer instruction meeting of their 2015 season—just an hour before Miranda pushed little Andres into the waves, hoping to see him stand on a surfboard for the first time.

"After we pair you into teams, you'll do a little ground instruction," she said, speaking to the group of volunteers who would soon be in charge of taking children with autism and other disabilities for a day of surfing in Deerfield Beach, Florida.

"We try to do it with every child, even though it's chaotic at the water line," she continued. "When starting that initial communication with the participant, kneel down at their level. Talk with them; introduce yourself to the child and the parent. Be sure to take off your sunglasses so they can see that vulnerability; that tells them you're here for them."

Then she spoke about the best language to use with the children: "You'll see many shirts around the beach that we made with our saying, 'Paddle, Paddle, Paddle, Up, Up, Up!' We use direct words so the participants are only hearing this one statement." I briefly scanned the crowd, now noticing blue shirts proudly emblazoned with this same saying. "Hopefully, at the end of the day, every participant will be doing this."

Although co-founder Don Ryan usually speaks at such meetings, this time he delegated the duties to Monica, knowing that she would speak from the heart. She's seen the true face of autism—during her eight years volunteering with SFA Surf Tours, she's witnessed firsthand how surfing can have therapeutic effects.

At previous SFA events, Monica has served as the tone setter. Working as a middleman at the waterline, she meets the participants and their parents, pairing each child up with a team of waiting volunteers. During event days, she laughs, sings, dances, runs; at every post-event after-party, she rarely has any voice left but always has a smile.

As she spoke, the beach and streets were growing more crowded and more loud by the minute. The sound of firetrucks and police cars filled the air, as they prepared to showcase their vehicles for the special needs participants.

Only a few minutes after Monica adjourned the assembly, the waterline was crowded and loud with bustle and chatter. Most of the 300 volunteers stood in line, parallel with the churning sea; each wore a colored wristband, dividing them into their respective sessions. The participant line, where the families and children filed in, was also full, arranged perpendicular to the water. Monica stood at the intersection in a bright yellow shirt emblazoned with "BEACH MARSHAL." As soon as another beach marshal blew an airhorn to signify the start of the first session of the 2015 season, Monica exploded with energy, and quickly began playing matchmaker, introducing participants to surf instructor volunteers and vice versa.

Given Miranda's tenure, she serves as an outlet for any young children that new or first-time volunteers might not know how to handle.

Monica connected us with our first participant—a boy no older than six who refused to make eye contact. Even with my limited experience as a volunteer with Surfers for Autism, I had learned to recognize this as a characteristic of the disorder—it actually had nothing to do with his enthusiasm. After several sandy practice rounds of standing up on the board, he proudly verbalized the goal of the day: "When a wave comes, I stand!"

Waves in Deerfield Beach are seasonal; swell reports spike during the fall and winter seasons due to hurricanes and cold fronts, but the sea looks like an endless lake in the summer season. Now, in April, the sea was living up to its late spring reputation; there were some choppy waves, about knee to waist high in height—too small for avid surfers, but well-suited for the children and young teenagers participating.

For the duration of the 15-minute heat, Miranda continued pushing the participant's board into sweeping waves, watching as the boy would slowly pop up, riding each wave to the beach.

Because Miranda was pushing, my job was to stand near shore and swiftly collect the board and its delighted passenger before pushing him back out to Miranda, thereby creating a circuit. Neither of us was quite sure where he sat on the autism spectrum, but it seemed that autism was left on the beach because he fearlessly paddled and stood and surfed every time.

I was surprised. Before meeting the child, I'd mentally prepared myself for the worst—screaming, fighting, scratching, even biting. Not only had I seen other volunteers take participants out surfing under these and other similarly difficult circumstances, I had experienced it myself. But this boy was totally at peace in the water. Taking him away from the safe confines of land and his parents' grip didn't cause anxiety;

rather, it seemed to relax and rejuvenate him. It goes to show how each surf session is different for each participant—which only served to further remind me of just how wide the autism spectrum is.

When the horn sounded, signaling the end of the heat, Miranda pushed the boy on his last wave, before collecting him and the foam surfboard and smiling for a quick photo, which was likely to end up on Facebook before making it into a picture frame.

After a quick rest, Monica introduced us to our second participant: an adorable little girl with visible developmental disabilities. She was a bit sluggish in her movements, especially during Miranda's ground instruction. So, while the girl sat on the board, Miranda took her time rolling in the sand, showing her how to "Paddle, Paddle, Paddle, Up, Up, Up!" Miranda was patient and all smiles, and after a few more practice runs she walked with the girl—who showed some initial hesitation when her feet first touched water—into the sea. Miranda began convincing the girl to lay on the surfboard, but she only met with more hesitation. This is a significant challenge for the surf instructors and volunteers: how much should you challenge participants? Some might suffer a breakdown under any pressure, while for others it may be just the fuel they need. Miranda walked this tightrope perfectly, softly speaking to the girl and convincing her to get onto the surfboard.

Another volunteer joined us, standing in the catching position near shore. I held the board steady in the water until a sizable wave came. At that point Miranda took over, hopping on the back of the board behind the participant, and paddling, kicking, and riding the whitewash all the way into shore, about 15 or 20 yards away.

When I later asked why Miranda chose to ride with the girl instead of push, as we did with the previous participant, she said that, given the girl's tiny frame, the added weight helped keep the nose of the board from sinking into the shallow water, which would in turn plummet the already nervous girl into the salty drink. After all, one wipeout can instantly cause a participant, who was previously making profound progress, to act on their anxiety and immediately exit the water, too fearful to return.

On every wave, instead of lying down on the board, the girl sat—as Miranda called it—"crisscross applesauce." Each time she plopped down onto the board, it looked as if she was preparing to slip down a water slide at Typhoon Lagoon in Orlando. Sitting upright with feet forward isn't the ideal surfing stance. So, pushing for progress, Miranda tried to get the girl to lie on her belly, just as she did during the beach instruction. But the moment Miranda tried to pick her up, the girl let out a dull moan that rapidly built into a loud screech. So Miranda allowed her to remain sitting down for a few more waves, with two or three minutes of rest in between, until the horn sounded. As Miranda waded with her back to shore, I noticed something was different about the girl. She had grown calmer and more confident throughout the heat.

Well aware that this was only the second session of between 12 to 15 heats slated for the entire day, Miranda mentioned that helping a participant achieve the goal of standing up on a surfboard "could come later in the day." The little girl's failure to stand was in no way a detriment. In fact, the girl trusting us, venturing into uncharted waters, and growing calmer, was incredible progress.

After we bid goodbye to the girl and her excited mother, it was time for us to meet our next participant. And, judging by Miranda's squeal, it was obvious she had a personal connection with him. While the other volunteer on our team walked down the beach to grab a surfboard, Miranda provided some background for me.

"My brother, Oliver, had a preschool teacher," she explained, "and she and my mom became good friends. She became pregnant, and my mom helped with the delivery. A few years later, her son was diagnosed. They knew about SFA, so they started coming to the events."

The young boy, whose name was Andres, quickly reached for Miranda's grip as soon as he joined us. He was adorable, sure to be a lady killer in the years to come, with his infectious smile, brown hair and brown eyes. Miranda somehow found a space of sand that wasn't already being used by other volunteers and participants and she began the beach instruction with Andres.

He looked happy, but it was clear he was nervous. "Lie on your belly, Andres—like this!" Miranda said, her stomach caked with Deerfield Beach's dark, loose sand. "Then, paddle as fast as you can!"

Andres followed the instructions, his tiny hands slowly scooping air and pushing it behind him, smiling and laughing all the while. And then, "Up, Up, Up! Stand up, Andres!" As he planted his sandy hands firmly on the board, his shoulders and chest rose, his knees followed, and he took one step, then another, until he stood tall in the surfing stance.

"Yes!" Miranda clapped. "Now let's practice one more time. Down on your belly. Now, as fast as you can! Faster! And up!"

Their goal clearly outlined, Miranda picked up Andres and I wrapped my arm around the eight-foot surfboard, weaving around other participants and volunteers with the sand sucking at my feet.

Miranda stopped me before I could wade beyond waist high water. "Let's keep him close to shore since he's so little," she explained. This way, apparently, he could catch waves that had already broken, ones that became small ripples of whitewash just big enough to ride.

Miranda plopped Andres on the board as I waded into ankle-deep water so that I could catch him and complete the circuit.

Wave after wave, he rode into the sand. I could hear his parents behind me clapping and cheering, but each time his feet touched land he would run to his father, who quickly turned him around by his shoulders and pushed him back towards the sea—and to me.

Andres was full of nervous joy, but we weren't sure why he wanted to stop surfing. "Has he ever stood on a wave?" I asked, as I met

Miranda close to shore to trade boy-for-board. "I'm not sure," she replied. "I don't think so. Today could be the first!"

Minutes later, she'd pushed the board into a wave and began chanting: "Up, Up, Up, Andres! Stand Up!"

Again, a five to eight-second belly ride ensued.

After a high five—his entire hand and fingers fit in my slippery palm—I towed him back towards Miranda. As I headed back to my original catching position, I could hear Miranda saying something to him, but I could not catch the words over the crashing of the waves. Plus, the 49 other children in the water—surrounded by many of the 300 volunteers at the day's event—were doing nothing to help the booming volume level.

I imagined that Miranda was talking to him about the goal: to stand, to surf, and about how incredible it would be for his parents to see him do something he's potentially never done before.

And moments later, as Miranda fired him in my direction and onto a coming wave, something clicked. He planted his hands as if he was about to stand up. His shoulders and chest lifted off the board and he looked like he was about to pull his knees to his chest to stand! But at that moment, he laid back down and finished the wave on his belly.

As I grabbed the board and pushed him back out to Miranda, I offered him an encouraging word: "You can do it! You can stand!" My heart was racing.

Minutes later, Miranda pushed him towards the shore and began to chant. Once again, Andres planted his hands on the board, his shoulders and chest lifted off the board and he looked as if he was about to… lie back down.

So again, I grabbed the board and pushed him in Miranda's direction. But just as Miranda's fingers touched the foam, the horn sounded for the end of the heat. It seemed like that goal would have to wait.

Unfazed, Miranda grabbed the board and flipped it around. Her facial muscles, usually so relaxed, were constricted. Her eyes, wide and beautiful, were now narrowed and focused, as her tone became sharp and serious. Even above the roar of the ocean and the crowd, I heard her say, "Andres, this is the last wave. You have to stand up this time. Okay?"

Moments later a wave came, and as she pushed him into whitewash she began to chant: "ANDRES, STAND UP! UP, UP, UP!"

Hands planted, his shoulders and chest rose. His knees followed, as he placed his two tiny feet firmly on the board with his torso lifted high. He was beaming as he barreled towards me and I could hear his parents going wild behind me on the beach.

Their excitement was nothing compared to Miranda, who charged towards the beach, kicking up gallons of saltwater and heaps of seaweed in the process. Seconds later, she had him in the air.

"ANDRES, YOU STOOD UP! YOU STOOD! YOU DID IT!"

"After the diagnosis, it was…a process. And it still is," Miranda's mother, Laura Fuentes, told me as we sat together near the Deerfield Beach pier, just a week before the first SFA event of the 2015 season. I'd been sent out by *Autism Parenting Magazine* to get the full story, and I was full of questions for the family.

I immediately took a liking to Laura and her husband, Alfie Fuentes. Although both were born and bred in the state of New York and only later came to call South Florida home, their accents aren't pronounced. They're the kind of parents that will invite you over for dinner, watch you fail in your attempt to wrap a burrito, and actually provide tips without embarrassing you.

When the family isn't at an SFA event, Alfie works 24-hour shifts as a firefighter; Laura is a full-time perinatal nurse. Thus, both of them see tough situations on a regular basis. They also have three children: Miranda, 17; Lucas, 15; and 10-year-old Oliver. All three take after their parents: brown eyes, curly hair, and a strong, surfer-like image. Together, you'd think nothing could break the Fuentes.

But autism certainly tried to.

We gazed out at the Deerfield Beach pier, which was lit by the full moon. I was about to find out the incredible significance the pier has for the family. Laura described Lucas' birth in 1999: "It was a normal delivery. Normal term, no complications. Developmentally, he was on target, and around 18 months, he began preschool. But then he started to regress in his vocabulary. He started showing all the typical autism traits. He wouldn't make eye contact…he began pulling back from the class."

"You have to realize there wasn't a whole lot of information out there about autism eleven or twelve years ago," Alfie interjected, sitting on the opposite side of Laura.

"It was a preschool teacher that brought our attention to a couple things," Laura went on. "Lucas wasn't talking that much, and within a couple of months he wasn't talking at all. He did everything in moans and grunts. We saw a psychologist, who ran a battery of tests for two or three weeks. Lucas was almost non-verbal by this point, so when he was given verbal tests he of course failed everything. The doctor said Lucas was moderately mentally retarded and uneducable, and he had some ADHD issues. He said it would get worse, too. That was the first anxiety attack I ever had."

She paused, listening to the sound of palm trees rustling above us from the cool night breeze. I could see the emotion in their eyes.

"When Lucas was three, he was in public school with severe speech, language and developmental delays," Laura continued. "We still hadn't really heard of autism. The school provided him with a language-based program that also targeted behavioral issues. When he turned five in 2004, he was potty trained and could say a couple of words, which was a definite improvement. His teacher said he would be okay to go to kindergarten, so he did.

"For the first half of that year…" She paused and took a deep breath. "He stared at the wall—that's all he did. During this time, he was still going through private therapy, which is where I saw a woman bringing in her son, who had autism. Some of the things I saw in him, I could see in Lucas. We put our heads together and later realized Lucas was—you know—staring at the wall. He was ticcing and stimming, too. That's when the woman asked me if Lucas had autism."

The terms "ticcing" and "stimming," already familiar now, had been completely new to me when I first started attending SFA events. Stimming is a body movement performed repeatedly; it's a nervous tic, a bad habit, something that everyone has—whether it's biting nails, cracking their knuckles, fidgeting, tapping their feet. But for those with autism, these behaviors are more pronounced, and include rocking back and forth, flapping their hands or making a noise. These happen for a myriad of reasons, such as excitement, anxiety, or as a means of self-comfort. When introducing those with autism to surfing, especially in front of crowds, it's easy to imagine why participants are often seen stimming.

Ticcing is similar to stimming; however, while medical literature says that stimming is somewhat suppressible, ticcing is not. Ticcing is a sudden, involuntary movement or sound, the most severe forms of which are known as Tourette's Syndrome.

Fighting the urge to stim in my own way by tapping my feet, I continued to stay silent, letting the conversation move forward at Laura's pace. That's another lesson gleaned from SFA events: when I don't have answers or advice (which is frequently), my rule of thumb is to show that I care by listening intently.

"First, there was denial," Laura said. "Lucas went through more testing, which came back with the diagnosis of autism. He finished the year in kindergarten, and we kept him in the first grade with Education Service Center services." She slowly shook her head. "It was horrifying! He was just another child to them. So we became even more aggressive, pulled him from the school, and placed him in a different school, one not mainstreamed.

"Lucas was in rough shape. Behaviorally he was at his worst, because now there's more confusion. He's older, but he has no idea how to respond to what people are telling him. We went to see a neurologist. Afterwards I was hysterical—crying all the time. Neurologists aren't psychiatrists. It's 'your kid has autism.' That's it; that's all you get."

Then, when a rigorous five-day-a-week speech and language therapy class began, things changed.

"See, Lucas repeated himself," Laura said. "He'd always done so. He couldn't pull out a new word; that was his struggle. Besides working on that, there was more education for us. We wondered, how had we not seen this? So there was guilt, and it overwhelmed us—the things you missed that you maybe should not have missed.

"At the same time, I was pregnant with Oliver, who is the best thing that ever happened to Lucas. Because of Oliver, Lucas has a best friend." She paused again, scanning the dark beach for her kids. I could make out Lucas' tall figure in the moonlight, with some little figure zooming around near him kicking up sand—presumably Oliver.

"Then, 2008 happened," I prodded, knowing Laura would take the bait. For frequent fliers—those who travel to each of the 10–13 events held during the annual Surf Tour—April 5, 2008 stands out: the date of the first-ever event.

Laura explained how, in late March 2008, a co-worker at the fire station mentioned to Alfie that an event was coming for children with autism and other special needs, one which included surfing at the Deerfield Beach Pier. Alfie was all ears.

"We attended with a lot of hesitation," admitted Laura. "Lucas was almost eight, and his autism was at its worst. At the time, we rarely went out as a family for fear of Lucas' behaviors, his tantrums and outbursts. We decided, with the help of my sister (Monica Valdes, who'd be leading the volunteer meeting at the Deerfield Beach event next week), that we would go. Miranda was ten at the time, and Oliver was three, so they came along.

"We had tried many activities with Lucas before, but so far nothing had interested him. Besides all of Lucas' typical autistic behaviors, I was worried that he would not understand the instructor. I remember wondering how surfers knew anything about autism...

"We arrived at the beach and the event was already in full swing. Everyone on the beach seemed happy—they were all smiles."

The family registered Lucas, and by the time the next horn sounded, the volunteers were ready to take him surfing. "They knelt down in front of him and said hello. Then they grabbed his hand and off they went," Laura recalled. "And that was it: no screaming, no meltdown, he just tiptoed along with them. We followed closely, watching the surfing instruction that takes place on the sand with the surfboard. Lucas, at the time, still barely spoke and I was afraid he wouldn't understand. None of that seemed to matter—not many words needed to be exchanged—and within minutes, Lucas was demonstrating what he had learned on the sand. He had learned to pop-up on the board, and he seemed to be at ease. Maybe it was the trusting hands and the kind faces of these two strange men; maybe it was the smell of the ocean air and the sand between his toes. All I know is within minutes my son was swept into the volunteer's arms and into the ocean without any tantrums or screaming."

Laura still remembers the feeling when she saw Lucas catch his first wave next to the Deerfield Beach pier. "The volunteer carefully placed him on the board and pushed it towards the shore, yelling, 'Up, Up, Up!' And that's exactly what Lucas did. He was standing and riding his first wave. The sense of accomplishment on his face said it all. As he came off the board, the volunteer hoisted him into the air, Lucas raised his hand in victory and the crowd cheered as I wept."

This moment was captured forever by a photo lens; today, the picture sits near the family computer in their house.

Laura continued, "The walls came down that day. We had seen a breakthrough; not only that, we'd seen humanity at its very best. Total strangers, giving so freely and lovingly of themselves for another."

She continued, "After all the day's activities and Lucas surfing multiple times, we met with Don and Kim Ryan, the co-founders of the event. We talked about why they do this, how the concept had evolved, and if they'd ever thought it would make parents like us feel this way. Their words and their excitement were contagious. Within minutes of our conversation after the event, we knew it was something we wanted to be a part of."

From that conversation with the Ryan's, Alfie and Laura learned that Surfers for Autism wasn't going to stay exclusive to Deerfield Beach; that the families who made up the organization wanted to take their surfboards up and down Florida's coast.

Today, the Surf Tour takes the form of an annual exodus to beach towns across Florida and Georgia, with each event spaced roughly three weeks apart. The event schedule comes out in late December, and events begin during April—the global autism-awareness month.

The 2015 season began in Deerfield Beach, and was slated to head north a few weekends later to Jupiter, FL. It then continued on to Stuart, Cocoa Beach, then went west across the state to St. Petersburg, then Ponce Inlet, Flagler Beach, Tybee Island, GA, Jacksonville Beach, and Naples, before wrapping things up in Ft. Myers on Halloween.

The Fuentes (including Laura's sister, Monica) planned to be at every event in 2015 so that Lucas could surf, Miranda could volunteer, and their youngest, the curly-haired Oliver, could be around some of his best friends.

Events also had special meaning to the youngest Fuentes, Oliver. "All of Oliver's friends are SFA participants," said Laura. "He goes around at every event and makes sure he says hello to everyone and has a deep interaction with his friends and their families.

"See, when Oliver was six, he wanted to surf at an event. We explained that this was a special day for kids with autism. He quickly named off a list of friends who were surfing, saying it was unfair, before breaking down in tears when he figured out they had autism. He then wiped his eyes and said it didn't matter, that they still were his best friends."

At each event, Laura and Alfie are executive level volunteers, not spectators. They are among the first on the beach and the last to leave, something which was particularly evident a week later during the first event of the 2015 season (at Deerfield Beach) when, before the sun had even risen above the water, Alfie was out driving an ATV, hauling equipment to the beach, while Laura organized the interior of the tents, helping with paperwork so the soon-to-arrive participants and volunteers could register.

Laura also shoulders food preparation responsibilities for some 1,500 participants, their families and volunteers during the day. Local restaurants donate meals, and she delegates.

"Never in our wildest dreams did we ever think that all of this would affect not only our kids, but everyone else that attends an event," said Laura. "Families, siblings, friends, communities…all united. United for one common cause."

During the afternoon surf sessions at Deerfield Beach, I learned that if there's a definition of SFA royalty, Miranda is it.

"Just wanted to say congratulations on your recent award," an older volunteer said to her just before we took out a blonde boy, who was so excited about surfing that he exploded into gibberish the second his feet hit the water. Miranda smiled and offered a small "Thanks," before quickly turning her attention back to our participant.

In between waves, she explained how she, her mother Laura and SFA co-founder Kim Ryan had flown to New York just weeks prior to the Deerfield Beach event before driving to Newtown, Connecticut, the site of the horrific school shooting in 2012 at Sandy Hook Elementary where six staff members and 20 children tragically lost their lives.

Their reason for visiting: a non-profit organization called Newtown Kindness, founded in memory of Charlotte Bacon, a precious six-year old who lost her life in the shooting, had nominated 28 teenagers nationwide for recognition of their own "acts of kindness." Miranda was to be honored for her eight-year volunteer service as a master surf instructor with SFA.

But that's only the tip of the iceberg. Back in 2013, Alfie and Laura started asking Miranda strange questions about her duties as a volunteer in preparation for a phone interview that had "something to do with Nickelodeon." Everything was kept hush-hush until the second-to-last SFA event that year, when a camera crew arrived at the beach and focused their lenses on her. Moments later, she was surprised by Austin Mahone, a renowned pop singer, who presented her with the news that she was receiving a Helping and Leading Others (HALO) award and would be flying out to Los Angeles to receive it at the TeenNick annual awards, known for having a viewership of millions.

"Two weeks after the event in Naples, they flew me out to California to see the Warner Brothers studio," she said, "and I met Shay Mitchell from *Pretty Little Liars*. Mom came with me that time. Then, two weeks later, I flew back again for the ceremony. Everyone came—Dad, Mom, Lucas, Oliver, Monica and Joe (Monica's soon-to-be husband). It was cool because I don't really get any attention for what I do, exactly, but at the same time too much attention makes me nervous."

It didn't help her nerves that the event was on live TV, but the anxiety never showed as she spoke on behalf of the non-profit about how surfing can be therapeutic, not only for the participants, but also for the volunteers like herself.

"At the after party, I met the executives of Nickelodeon and thought, 'I'm touching the person who's on top of all this!' It's scary. I talked to Austin again, met his manager, and also met Nick Cannon. Nick was cool. Chill! Funny."

The attention didn't stop there. Outlets like MTV, NBC Miami, the Miami Sun Sentinel, and more had coverage of Miranda's speech. But for her, it's clearly not about the awards or the ceremonies. It's always about the next participant; it's about a little blonde boy trying to stand on a surfboard in Deerfield Beach.

Carrying our participant back to shore after the heat ended, Miranda remarked how happy he seemed. Although she tried to get him to "Up, Up, Up," the boy continued to rattle off gibberish and stim as drool dripped from his chin. His eyes never stopped dancing, and he seemed happy enough being in the ocean, even though he was initially hesitant to enter the salty therapeutic arena. Again, I was struck by how progress can be made simply by venturing into the salty unknown.

By mid-afternoon, Miranda and I took a seat in the sand, feeling nothing short of exhausted. But the event showed no signs of slowing down—the beach remained crowded, still loud and alive with reggae music, while Monica kept running around as if it were still her first hour on the beach. I could feel the fatigue setting in my shoulders; I ached from carrying the eight-foot surfboards and picking up children. My feet felt sore from the uneven terrain, and my legs felt tight from running against the sinking sand.

So you can imagine my shock when Miranda suddenly jumped up, as she noticed Lucas walking towards the participant line. "Lucas is coming!" she screamed. I wearily followed in her sandy footprints, navigating my way through families and volunteers until I found a surfboard. When we met Lucas in the water, I was a bit worried that his lanky figure wouldn't fit on the surfboard, but he was quick to adjust, hopping on belly-first with ease. Miranda gave me the nod to take him out by myself while she stayed in to play catcher.

I pushed him out to where the waves were breaking. As we ventured deeper and deeper into the crowded drink, he kept swiveling his head from side to side, sizing up the scene. There were 49 other participants still being pushed into waves by a swarm of volunteers, still yelling the chant Monica had carefully explained hours ago.

I flipped Lucas around to face the shore and he began squinting, all of his teeth showing. At this point, his skin was still dry, and I saw he was shivering.

Swiveling my neck back towards the sea, I saw a wave coming in and gave Lucas the heads-up. "Okay Lucas, a perfect-sized wave is coming. Here we go!"

Right as the wave passed through us, I pushed.

I didn't have to say anything. No 'Up, Up, Up!' No 'Go, Go, Go!' I just watched.

Lucas' back rose above the wave and in one fluid movement he planted his hands on both sides of the board, pushing up quickly as his toes stuck to the foam. He was up and riding, taking the wave to the sand. Laura and Alfie were easily identifiable on the crowded shoreline, wearing their blue 'STAFF' t-shirts. I could see they were cheering. Like watching a pro quarterback throw a football in person, the swiftness and ease of Lucas's movement was a sight to behold.

He paddled back to me on his own, ready for another wave. Because he'd been quiet so far, I tried to start a conversation, remembering that he loved all things *Pirates of the Caribbean*.

"Hey Lucas, did any of the *Pirates of the Caribbean* characters surf?" I asked. I was curious if he favored one character in particular.

Lucas snapped his head towards me and stared me straight in the eyes.

"No, they never did," he answered.

"But what about Davy Jones, from the second film?" *I think?* "I bet he surfed on some of the islands they went to."

"He never did! No, he never," Lucas replied.

"Not even when they wanted to take a break from the Black Pearl ship?"

"No, they didn't."

I laughed and excitedly said, "Okay, here's another wave, Lucas!"

I pushed, and again watched as Lucas caught the wave and popped up: his hands planted, chest rising and his legs slid into perfect position. And there he was—up perfectly and swiftly. He rode the wave into the sand with his family still watching proudly.

It wasn't until Lucas started paddling back, again on his own power, that the realizations started flooding in. Here was a boy who could only repeat words, now holding conversations. A boy who had difficulty finding interests, now an incredible surfer. A boy battling to graduate from elementary school, now a great 15-year-old student.

I pushed him into another wave. And another. And another. I watched him as if there was no one else in the water, until the horn sounded and snapped me out of my tear-inducing thoughts.

As the day wore on, my exhaustion continued to slow me down. My exercise routine of surfing, running and hitting the gym didn't do much to prepare me for a 7–8-hour adrenaline and emotion-fueled day in the sand and sun. I was already feeling sore, but I at least didn't have any sunburn, thanks to a long-sleeve rash guard and a large straw hat. Oddly enough it was my face that hurt the most; I had no idea why my jaw muscles were so sore.

Even though it seemed that Miranda had an endless amount of energy, she does have certain limitations that even passion and drive can't overcome. At events, this relegates her to smaller participants. When larger or older participants stand tall in the participant line, waiting for a team of volunteers to take them surfing, Monica looks for men—big men—to handle them. Men who don't care if their skin gets scratched, or their hair pulled, or their crotch punched.

Men like Byron Anderson.

Earlier in the morning, when the Deerfield Beach sand was still feeling cool on my feet, Miranda and I were about to take a little girl into the water when we heard Monica yelling, "I need two big guys! I need two big guys!"

This was followed by a loud, high-pitched scream. Beside the participant chute, a large boy was in full panic mode. The boy, who I guessed to be around 12 or 13 years old, was using his 100 plus-pound figure to his advantage. His hands were slapping the air and beating the sand, which spewed out in all directions. More troubling, he wouldn't stop hitting himself in the head.

I had no clue as to why he was having a meltdown. It could have been the noise of the beach, the unfamiliar environment, the prospect of meeting new people, or venturing into uncharted territory. Either way, autism had full control of him.

Monica ran in front of us, yelling again for big guys, when a voice behind us boomed: "I'm here! I'm here!"

I turned, and there was Byron.

When you first see him, you'd initially think that he's of Samoan or Hawaiian descent. He has dark eyes, a buzzed head, a confident walk and a fast gait. Moreover, he looks *very* strong, almost to the point of invincibility. While you can see Alfie Fuentes' strength in individual features—in his shoulders, neck, torso—Byron looks like one big ball of muscle. I'd be shocked if he didn't play (and excel at) high school football.

Byron ran to the boy, sand kicking up behind him, followed by Keith Arnold, a volunteer equally strong as Byron and whose son is an SFA frequent flier. The boy's mother stepped away and Byron and Keith hoisted him to his feet as if he weighed nothing. They then sprinted towards the water line with the boy in tow, still screaming, where two more volunteers were waiting with one of SFA's bigger surfboards—a ten-foot yellow board.

The boy continued to wail as they took him out; I kept watching until Monica's voice snapped my focus back to the chute. She was continuing to hand out more participants to volunteers, but most of the 30 or 40 volunteers around me were staring as Byron tried to get the boy to lie on the board.

There was no judgment in the eyes of those who watched. Some had hands over their mouths; some had wet eyes; others watched in awe. A few smiled. The boy's mother, who was standing above us on the beach incline, had tears in her eyes as she watched.

We lost sight of Bryon, Keith and the boy as the heat continued, but I did notice his cries stopped echoing a few minutes afterwards.

Later, Byron told me that the boy stopped biting and hitting himself during the session. "When we took the boy in," he said, "the mother actually called me a saint."

Sunday morning, 11 a.m. Families slowly trickled onto the beach to say goodbye to Don and Kim Ryan, both standing by the SFA tents perched on the beach. The previous day's activities were enough to sap anyone's energy, and the after-party had kept everyone out late. The city had closed the street above the beach area, and it was filled with crowds watching the live bands that SFA brought to town. Children with special needs danced freely, beer and other refreshments were everywhere, and parents had a chance to let loose.

Making my way to grab some early lunch at one of the five food trucks still standing after last night's events, I noticed Byron already eating, while talking with a volunteer from the previous day.

We three began discussing our battle scars—sunburns, blisters, scrapes and the strange ache in my jaw. Byron pointed to his right arm, where teeth marks were still clearly visible.

"We had a few biters yesterday," he said, laughing. "I actually thought it was a jellyfish wrapped around my arm, but nope! It was a kid we were taking out. Could have been the boy me and Keith grabbed when he was having a tantrum on the beach."

He scanned his other arm and pointed. "But see this mark here?" he asked. "Yeah," he continued, nodding, "that's definitely a bite mark."

2
DIAGNOSIS

"You try to think long term—will my child ever go to college? Live alone? Will he ever have a career? Can she ever find love and have kids of her own? But you dismiss those thoughts because your boy is now five and having a tantrum in front of the Cinderella Castle at Disney World and everyone is staring so that's all you have time to focus on."

At first, I thought there had to be something in the Kool-Aid. How else can you explain a collection of families, whose only commonality is being in some way touched by autism and other disabilities, spending their precious vacation days at weekend surf events up and down Florida's coast, year after year?

I didn't get it. And I certainly didn't get autism; it's something that I had never been exposed to. I happened to hear about an event called Surfers for Autism taking place a few hours north of my South Florida location in Jacksonville Beach. I went to ask some questions, take some pictures, and volunteer; after an eight-hour beach day, I returned with a collection of photos and sound bites, sore shoulders, and a feeling of actually making a difference.

From then on, year after year, I attended events and wrote for numerous publications about SFA events. Each article followed the same winning format: it began with a heartwarming moment of a teary-eyed mother watching her child surf, before zooming out to cover the who/what/when/where and why of the event, before wrapping it all up with quotes from co-founder Don Ryan, Miranda Fuentes and other volunteers about these "life-changing" events.

The writing became routine. I felt the repetition of my formula was diluting the emotions of the event—the tears, the laughs and the smiles. Something was lost in translation.

With this realization came a question—one which quickly became a challenge: is there more to this story? What truly motivates these families—some of whom have completed this circuit every year for over a decade—to follow this program up and down the coast? Is it the therapeutic aspects of surfing? The friendships and sense of community they've found there?

Above all else, the overarching question that drove my curiosity was this: *how* is surfing therapeutic for the participants?

I realized that the only way to truly find out the answers to these questions was to drink the Kool-Aid—to go all-in, without reservation, like downing a shot. For one year, I would attend as many SFA events as possible and shadow the core "frequent flier" families, spending time at every event with a new family. I would learn their stories of struggles and successes, I would help their children surf, and I would carefully watch for breakthroughs.

It was decided, then. I would give myself completely to the cause, to the families, to helping, and see what I could see.

The first step was picking up the 2015 SFA schedule, an itinerary stretching coast to coast from April to October:

4/10–4/12: 8th Annual South Florida SFA Beach Festival
[DEERFIELD BEACH]

5/9:	6th Annual SFA Beach Festival of the Palm Beaches [JUPITER]
5/30:	7th Annual Treasure Coast SFA Beach Festival [STUART BEACH]
6/20:	7th Annual Space Coast SFA Beach Festival [COCOA BEACH]
7/11:	5th Annual Bay Area SFA Beach Festival [ST. PETE BEACH]
8/1:	6th Annual Inlet SFA Beach Festival [PONCE INLET]
8/22:	6th Annual First Coast SFA Beach Festival [FLAGLER BEACH]
9/12:	5th Annual Coastal Empire SFA Beach Festival [TYBEE ISLAND]
9/26:	6th Annual North Coast SFA Beach Festival [JACKSONVILLE BEACH]
10/17:	4th Annual Everglades SFA Beach Festival [NAPLES]
10/31: 5	th Annual Gulf Coast SFA Beach Festival [FT. MYERS]

Since attending my first event in 2010, I'd often heard that the main draw to the surf sessions, besides giving children with autism the chance to surf or allowing families to relax in a judgment-free environment, was the breakthroughs—the progress made in breaking down the concrete walls around these children, until every barrier crumbled and disintegrated into the sea.

After spending time with families dedicated to the surf therapy cause, I noticed that when these breakthroughs happen, both on the surfboard and in the sand, they provide parents and therapists with another piece to the puzzle that is their child's individual form of autism.

But "puzzle" isn't quite the right word. After all, puzzles by nature are objective. There is only a handful of pieces and every piece has a place; if one is missing, its absence is clearly evident by the hole left in the picture. There are never extra pieces, and when all's said and done, there's a completed image formed. Easy. Simple, even—a game meant for children. Unfortunately, society's presentation of puzzles as a game doesn't do autism any favors in the comparison.

Imagine that you've just spent the past 9 months anticipating the birth of your beloved child. For a few years, your little boy or little girl babbles their first words, grows hair, makes eye contact, responds to your commands, begins to crawl and even starts walking. Your hopes and dreams for them grow by the day. You imagine that your child will be anything they desire: a politician, a lawyer, an actor.

Unfortunately, while some developmental disorders are hinted at before birth, most aren't revealed in full until a child's developmental stage. You, as their parent, notice the problem first: signs of regression. You won't remember when things started, but something seems... *different* about your child. He's not making as much eye contact as he once did. It takes an extra command to get her to listen. At preschool, their teachers may notice withdrawal factors. He's not interacting with classmates. She seems to be in her own world, and the teacher has to repeatedly snap her out of it.

You write it off, at first. It's probably growing pains, right? Friends will tell you, "You're reading into it too deeply, thinking too much."

You believe them—why wouldn't you—and try to brush off the anxiety.

But then it gets worse. It becomes evident that the terrible twos aren't a phase for your child—it's their everyday life. Eye contact has dwindled to nothing. It's almost as if your little girl isn't listening to you at all. Maybe that's normal, you think. Or maybe it's early signs of ADHD? Should you get her hearing checked?

Eventually, something kicks you into action and you make an appointment with a doctor. The motive factor is different for everyone;

maybe it's the tantrums, or the fear of thinking something is wrong. Maybe you're just frustrated that your child isn't listening to you.

And so you find yourself sitting in a clean-tiled waiting room. Autism is the last thing on your mind, but after a battery of tests, which can range from days to weeks, it's the first word out of the doctor's mouth. That six-letter word forever places your child into a statistical category.

Autism. Your child is on the autism spectrum. The diagnosis is objective, it's factual—it's reality.

And now it's a part of *your* life.

Thoughts and emotions begin flooding your brain. Anger—at yourself, for not seeing the signs, for not even knowing the signs; frustration—at how long these tests have taken, at how the doctor is spelling out these hard, cold facts with little sympathy; or fear—of the label, fear of how your child is going to be looked at now that he has autism.

Denial kicks in. What do these doctors and their tests know, anyway? Or else anxiety takes hold: how are you supposed to handle your child, who seems like a completely different person now? How will you pay for these tests, let alone the therapy this white coat is recommending?

For some, the tears happen in front of the doctor. Others wait until they hit fresh air. Some bury it completely, setting it aside to deal with at a later moment.

After you leave the doctor's office and put your child down for the night, you try to rally. You jump on the internet and start looking for those puzzle pieces, scrolling through page after page, searching for anything that can help.

One of the first sources that'll pop up in front of your drooping eyes is the Center for Disease Control and Prevention's website. They provide a mouthful of a definition for autism:

A developmental disability that can cause significant social, communication and behavioral challenges. There is often nothing about how people with ASD (Autism Spectrum Disorder) look that sets them apart from other people, but people with ASD may communicate, interact, behave and learn in ways that are different from most other people. The learning, thinking, and problem-solving abilities of people with ASD can range from gifted to severely challenged. Some people with ASD need a lot of help in their daily lives; others need less.[1]

It sounds so generic to your ears. And you notice that it says a lot without really saying anything helpful. You continue scrolling down the page, looking for symptoms.

Children or adults with ASD might avoid eye contact and want to be alone, prefer not to be held or cuddled, or might cuddle only when they want to, or lose skills they once had (for example, stop saying words they were using).[2]

No comfort there, then. You find another website called Autism Speaks that lists more symptoms, such as "repetitive behaviors, genetic disorders, seizures, sleep dysfunction."[3]

What's the typical age of diagnosis of this thing called autism, you wonder? How many signs did you miss? Could you have caught it sooner? A click reveals the answer: "Even though ASD can be diagnosed as early as age 2 years, most children are not diagnosed with ASD until after age 4 years."[4]

Hungry for a different source, you trace your web search back to Autism Speaks, which explains the prevalence of autism: 1 in 42 boys, and 1 in 189 girls.[5]

You keep digging, coming across a website called Autism Society, and your mouth drops: "The prevalence of Autism in U.S. children increased by 119.4 percent from 2000 (1 in 150) to 2010 (1 in 68), a finding initially by the CDC."[6]

Tired of statistics, you come across commentary that says the numbers aren't painting a clear picture, that doctors and therapists are just now testing for autism when they haven't in decades and centuries past. But that does little to calm your stress; it does nothing to change the fact that your child is now part of the number.

Turning the computer off and sitting in the silence, you realize that now you must determine not only where the pieces go in the puzzle that is your boy or your girl; you also have to find the pieces all by yourself.

But where do you start? Loud noises, for example: sometimes those can bother your girl. Or, are there certain foods that upset your boy's stomach, leading to meltdowns and tantrums? There's another piece.

Therapies have their own pieces, as well. Before you can know which therapies work for your child specifically, you have to try them out, including those the doctors recommended and maybe even some they didn't. One may work, others won't; but it will take weeks and many co-pays to find out. And the end result of all the bills, phone calls and car rides is just a few more pieces to the puzzle.

So you start collecting these pieces and try to fit them together. You become your little girl's biggest advocate, because who else will take on that kind of 24-hour-a-day, 7-days-a-week job?

Because despite the tantrums or the silence, you know she's in there, somewhere; underneath the brown hair and behind those big green eyes in your baby.

They say life is about the journey, not about the destination. But whoever said that never dealt with autism. With autism, there are no destinations, only an endless journey. Having a partner helps with the workload; but sometimes exhaustion, stress and bitterness—especially when you see the bills—begin to build. It knocks at the front door when you're least expecting it. Suddenly that promise both of you made years ago seems like centuries ago, and in the place of attraction, beach walks, and words of affirmation is nothing but stress without end. You start to understand why people say that the divorce rate among couples with special needs children is so high. Doubt follows in your footsteps, haunting your daily routine like a ghost.

Yet another difficulty with the puzzle of autism is that you don't begin with an end goal in mind—only a hope for what it may look like. You try to think long term—will my child ever go to college? Live alone? Will he ever have a career? Can she ever find love and have kids of her own? However, you dismiss those thoughts because your boy is now five and having a tantrum in front of the Cinderella Castle at Disney World and everyone is staring, so that's all you have time to focus on.

There's also the ever-present probability that the puzzle will never be completed. As the doctor told you, there is no current "cure," as we still don't know what causes autism. You've heard of autism walks and autism therapies and such by now, but now this word "cure" is starting to upset you. Who's to say that your child needs "curing" from his current "condition"?

So what if he likes to run around the house naked? So what if her best friend is her service dog? Do those actions need "curing," too? Given the behavioral implications of autism, the term "normal" begins to sound more subjective than ever before.

Not helping matters is how the puzzle pieces…well, just aren't consistent. You may get three clues to what helps or bothers your child in a single week, and then go cold for a year. You may have trouble knowing which pieces to keep and which to throw away; reading behavioral trends takes weeks, even months, or perhaps years to monitor. With so much going on, it can be difficult to remember these trends or find that piece of paper that has all your notes. After all, when your little girl throws a tantrum, a whirlwind of objects hit the floor. Items are bound to get lost during the cleanup.

An even bigger piece to the puzzle is school. Do you mainstream your child? Will the public schools offer better services? Even if private school is better, is it affordable? If your boy is mainstreamed, can he keep up? Will there be bullying? If your little girl is put into classes with other special needs children, will she be challenged enough? Can you trust the teachers? Can you trust the school system?

What about going out in public? Perhaps your little boy can't sit in a restaurant without squirming. The looks you get from taking your girl to the grocery store are sometimes unbearable.

Or the comments:

"Get control of your kid."

"Why don't you discipline her?"

"You're causing other customers to feel uncomfortable."

It is heartbreaking and frustrating—and it's even more pieces to the puzzle, knowing where you can and can't go.

On your daily commute, you keep seeing that billboard for a vacation cruise, beckoning to you. Remember how you wanted to take your family to those perfect beaches in the Bahamas? Now, you're not so sure he can sit still on an airplane. And there's certainly no way he's going to like those strange men and women in the blue uniforms at the airport asking everyone to take off their shoes.

Time begins to blur. Christmas comes sooner than last year, and now summer is already here. Your little girl may be ticcing and stimming, but that doesn't keep you from buying her a training bra. In the quiet times, you wonder if you'll be able to place a photo of her going to prom on your desk at work. You start to notice hints of fuzz on your boy's face, and your wife puts photos on Facebook of you teaching him how to shave for the first time.

That's when you realize that hormones change the game completely. Your boy's stronger and taller, now. Your neighbors ask why, every time they come over to your house, you have the living room furniture moved around. "I like a change of scenery," you reply, when in reality the couch they're sitting on is covering holes in the wall—holes the exact size of your boy's hand.

Therapy remains as consistent as each day's sunrise, paying off in more and more puzzle pieces drifting into focus. And you celebrate each and every one; there are the dance parties in the kitchen, surprise visits to theme parks, videos shared online. Eventually you get to feeling as though things have stabilized somewhat, and you're thankful that the foundation of progress is already built.

Now it's time to shoot for the stars, right?

Your daughter's therapist starts asking if you've explained to your child what happens after high school. "*Am I supposed to have her dream big, only to be let down?*" you think on the drive back home. "*Do I tell her to aim low? Can she find a job, much less keep it? Where do I set the bar?*"

Your partner reminds you that the future is not something to fear; that it's simply a collection of the decisions made yesterday and today. But all the water-cooler talk at work about "empty nester" benefits is something you know you may never experience. As a parent, you know that your child can't live on his own. You look at your girl, and even as you marvel at her beauty, you think about a white dress and the walk down the aisle. And you wonder. You think. You dream.

You realize why mid-life crises exist, but there's no time for you to entertain such thoughts. Every year, you see more and more grey hairs and you start seriously pondering your mortality. "*What will she be like if I'm not here? Can someone take care of him when I'm gone? If I leave him any money, the state-funded programs may not help him. And what about...when I need to be taken care of?*"

But what can you do? You breathe. Breathe. Breathe. And the second you walk into the house your little girl takes your breath away. Because you realize how she's not a little girl anymore; she is a woman, and she is ticcing, and she is beautiful.

You never told your wife or your children, but one or two of those holes in the wall are actually yours. Because this puzzle just won't stop eating at you. Nothing is worse than regret, and its ice-cold grip has you constantly second-guessing your actions. You and your wife talk about it—the money, the therapists, the schools—and you remember why you married her. She reminds you that life is something that only moves forward, never backwards; that you made the best decisions you could, with the amount of information you had at the time.

How could you have known that therapy wouldn't have helped? Or that the school system would have created so many frustrations?

And it's only when the lights in the house go out and everyone is asleep, that you think the thoughts you fight against and rarely entertain.

What if the autism didn't exist?

But then your logic kicks in. When it comes to talking about hopes for your kids, there's really not much difference between parents of children with special needs and parents of those that are "typical."

You want your girl to be happy. You want your boy, who now stands at 5'9", to smile every day.

Parents who don't face autism want that same thing.

And today, she *was* happy. He *did* have fun today.

And it's the thought of that smiling face that stays with you as your body goes still and you drift off to sleep into the quiet night.

3

THE WHEEL OF AUTISM

"So Santa looks at me and says, 'You should have your son tested for autism.' And I said, 'Who...who the hell are you to tell me that?'"

A visit to see Santa Claus in a Boca Raton mall in December 2007 changed everything for the Weppner family.

After Michele made breakfast for her husband, Chris, and her two boys, Daniel and Nate, the whole family of four packed themselves into the car with their sights set on the mall. Michele couldn't quite put her finger on it, but throughout the last week Nate, her youngest, had been acting...strange. Something seemed off. She chalked it up to her overthinking things and focused instead on how much time a visit to Santa would take (which would determine how much time she would have to complete her Christmas shopping).

They waited in line, and when it was Nate's turn, Santa hoisted him up and did his jolly routine as usual. But St. Nick noticed something.

"So Santa looks at me and says, 'You should have your son tested for autism,'" Michele recalls. "And I said, 'Who...who the hell are you to tell me that?'"

She told me this while I sat in the living room of her Boca Raton home, her voice on an elevator that only went up.

She continued: "At the time I thought, 'He's just...distracted! He's a little boy!' But my older son, Daniel, didn't act this way at that age.

"Later, I took him to see our pediatrician, who is an older woman— she said, 'He'll outgrow it.' We started to think he had hearing problems, because he wouldn't respond to anything we said. We had no idea what was going on. He wouldn't make eye contact like he used to. Then, we're watching a doctor trying to interact with him, and I'm standing there saying, 'Oh my god...he's got it. My Nate has autism.' That was April 17, 2008. I will never forget that day."

She also won't forget the odd timing in Nate's regression. Abruptly standing up from the couch, Michelle grabbed two photo frames off the wall and handed them to me.

I looked at the first photo. It was adorable baby Nate! He had a beautiful face and soft skin, blonde hair and blue eyes; he didn't look much older than 1 year old in the picture. He appeared happy and attentive.

"See how he's looking at the camera?" his mother said, smiling. Then the smile vanished. "Now, compare it to this," her voice suddenly dark, while she handed me the second frame. Another picture of Nate; this time he wasn't looking at the camera. What's more, he looked uncomfortable in his own skin, and it seemed like a heavy fog had drifted over his eyes that he couldn't peer through. He didn't look focused, either; something was definitely different.

"See how, in this photo, he has more buck teeth?" she pointed out.

I nodded. "What happened in between these?"

She looked me direct in the face and took a deep breath, before saying, "The second photo was after his MMR vaccination."

Her tone shifted to one of protective authority. Michele Weppner talks like she moves—quickly and purposefully. "Nate had the shot at two, like everyone else. Afterwards, he started walking on his tippy toes.

His belly extended, then he started having digestion problems, along with sleeping problems…anytime there would be a full moon, he was awake. I had no idea what was happening. Sometimes I still don't."

With that, she was done talking about the vaccine controversy, which is still a hot button topic on media platforms today. It's public knowledge that scientists and governmental officials continue to insist that the vaccines we give to our children are indeed safe, but there are still frequent questions, debates, and protests from those who claim to have experienced specific changes firsthand.

Michele isn't exactly sure how the fog of autism infiltrated her boy's eyes, but she does know that time spent thinking about it won't prevent Nate's next meltdown or outburst. Nostalgia is reserved for those who don't want to look forward; her motivation, her direction, is today first, tomorrow afterwards.

Even though she was initially green to autism's intricacies, Michele became Nate's biggest advocate overnight, scheduling appointments for Applied Behavior Analysis (ABA) therapy, shifting the family savings around to accommodate the cost of treatment, and all the while cooking, cleaning and trying to maintain some semblance of normalcy in her household. Asking how work was for her husband, Chris, taking Daniel to school—just trying to keep it all together.

Ask Michele which errands are the most difficult, and she'll tell you it's the weekly grocery store runs, where Nate would knock items off the shelves on accident, flailing his arms, grabbing and pulling. With one hand clasping his tiny fingers and another holding the shopping cart, her phone, her shopping list and her wallet, she still had time to notice people staring at him, at the candy littered down the aisles, then back at him, before turning their glares on her.

Michele recalled one trip in particular that, like a visit to the chiropractor, popped her back into place. A year after Nate's diagnosis, she was strolling out of a Target when she saw a piece of paper inserted under her car's windshield wipers. Praying that it wasn't a parking ticket, she freed one hand from under a heavy bag of groceries and slipped the paper out.

As she scanned the page, it suddenly felt like the big man upstairs had stepped off a cloud, come down to earth, and given her a kiss.

Rather than a parking ticket, it turned out to be a flyer describing something called "Surfers for Autism."

Instead of driving home, Michele waited in the parking lot for over an hour to meet whoever had placed this godsend in front of her eyes. It turned out to be none other than SFA co-founder Don Ryan.

The organization had just had their first event about a week ago at Deerfield Beach pier, which wasn't too far from the Weppner house, and Don was out spreading the word. But before Don could even finish speaking about the Fuentes, or the tents, or the breakthroughs they'd seen, Michele was fired up. She couldn't wait to tell Chris, Daniel, and especially Nate the good news.

They would be at one of the upcoming events, no if's, and's, or but's.

Just hearing the list of beach towns the program would be visiting sounded like a vacation. She knew Nate struggled with public playgrounds, malls, restaurants, and amusement parks—but who needs all that when you can surf?

When she got home and told her family the good news, Nate responded by moaning a combination of "oohs" and "ahhs." And somehow, someway, Michele knew that despite the non-verbal label, he'd heard her.

Tell Nate's therapist this story, and she'd probably chalk it up to a result of Nate's ABA (Applied Behavioral Analysis) therapy. Her official title is a Senior Consultant M.ED BCBA (Board Certified Behavior Analyst), but given the time she's been with Nate, her only title inside the Weppner household is that of family.

"When I first met Nate almost two years ago," she told me, "he was highly resistant to the therapeutic activities presented to him and frequently resorted to physical aggression that resulted in tissue damage to therapists who had previously worked with him."

Complicating matters, neither Michele nor the therapists she took Nate to were sure how much he was actually retaining from his sessions. But Michele pushed the pedal to the floor regardless, scheduling as much therapy as her insurance company would allow, praying for and anticipating the puzzle pieces to follow.

In order to gain more understanding about the journey that is ABA therapy, I sat in on one of Nate's sessions on a warm February morning. This was about two months before the first event of the 2015 season at Deerfield Beach, where Miranda would see Andres standing on his first wave.

I sat in-between the therapist and Michele as we watched Nate make a circuit of the yard. He followed a strict path: first jumping off the trampoline, running beside the pool, then away from the pool, then jumping on an upside-down eight-foot surfboard, and finally back to the trampoline. He did this over and over again.

Nate's therapist explained that he'd recently started repeating noises and words that he heard from Michele, an act that autism can inhibit in some cases.

"If you think about it, when you were young your first words were imitations of your parents," the therapist said. "You heard and saw them use a word for an object, and you repeated that. With autism, that can be more difficult to do. As a child with autism grows older, you start to see that social cues aren't being understood as well. In ABA therapy, we work on that: we become that inner voice, saying what they should be thinking. We consistently increase words and sounds."

The day's therapy session, like always, was a four-hour long affair, and even though it was only 8:30 a.m. Michele's eyes already looked exhausted. Earlier, when she'd opened the front door, she greeted me with, "I've been up since 4:30 this morning." This was before Nate flashed behind her and she was off to catch him again.

Michele's eyes followed Nate and his circuit in the backyard.

"Autism is almost like a wheel of fortune," she confided. "You have all these feelings on this big wheel and every morning you just spin it and see what it lands on. That's how the therapist first described it to me, and it makes so much sense."

While we talked, the therapist worked diligently on her computer, writing up critiques for another therapist who had been trailing Nate the entire time in the backyard. As we continued watching, Michele asked the therapist what her predictions were for when Nate would begin noticing girls.

Which is yet another daunting piece of the puzzle, one that I had only recently begun thinking about: Do you allow children on the spectrum to have thoughts of sex? Of having children? If not, should you look to stymie their hormones? Is it even your place to do so? Just as I was about to ask Michele these questions, she stepped inside the house to make a snack for Nate.

Nate plopped into "his" chair and sat on his ankles, oohing in energetic bursts, as Michele brought him a bowl of vegetables, explaining that this was his third meal today, even though it wasn't even 10 a.m. Leaving the bowl in Nate's reach, she headed back into the kitchen, where she re-tied the fabric ropes that locked the fridge and pantry doors shut.

Nate reached out to grab a handful of greens, until the other therapist cheerfully reminded him, "No, Nate, use your fork, remember?"

Nate obediently picked up the fork with his left hand, placed a pea in his mouth, and began chewing loudly, chomping and smacking, oohing and ahhing.

"Since we're in his house, he doesn't care about manners," said Michele, laughing.

He also didn't care about being clothed, typically.

But the day was two hours gone and his clothes were still on, so it seemed like things were going well so far. Although, when the therapist turned to converse with Michele a few minutes later, Nate quickly forced his right hand into the bowl, snatching up a carrot with his fingers. When the helper turned around to see the rule being broken, she cajoled him with, "No Nate, please use the fork." He quickly picked it back up, and after finishing his snack, we went back outside.

Where, despite being fully clothed, he bolted immediately for the pool.

Just as he crept near the edge, the therapist yelled, "Stop, Nate!" He *did* stop, and settled for peering over the edge, eyeing his reflection in the calm water. Satisfied, he turned around and went back to his circuit.

Michele was grinning from ear to ear. "See, there are so many times when, even though he may *want* to stop, or sit, or come here as he's told, he can't, because he's simply overwhelmed," explained the therapist, keeping a close eye on Nate. "But today he's responding well."

Nate zipped back onto his circuit, finally breaking it to venture near us. He approached Michele and pushed his forehead onto hers.

What followed can only be described as a mother and son moment and is perhaps the reason why adults have children in the first place. Nate made eye contact with his mother, blue eyes on blue, listening as she said over and over again, "I love you, Nate! I love you, Nate!" The smile that appeared on his face spread to his cheeks and ears as their noses touched. He laughed, followed by an especially long, "Ooooh."

Next, he tiptoed towards me and started patting my head, while he looked off into the distance. I didn't know what to do or say, so I elected to just smile and remain quiet.

"See, he knows you more!" said Michele. The therapist nodded in agreement.

Just then, Nate slowly walked behind us and, in one swift motion, he opened the sliding door and jumped inside. Two loud bangs followed. It sounded like the pantry doors.

"I don't know why he's been upset off and on today," Michele said, looking worried.

Another bang came from inside, and Michele quietly stood, favoring one leg, pulled herself together and stepped into the house. The therapist took one look inside and said, "His clothes are coming off!" before stepping into the battle.

"It was the food," Michele said. It was about 10 minutes later, and we were gathered in the living room. Michele was having a conversation with the therapist, while my eyes wandered around the room, eventually landing on Nate's contrasting baby photos.

"One thing we've learned is that saying 'No' creates anxiety," said the therapist. "Nate may think that if I say 'No' to his wanting, say, ice cream, that it means, 'No, you can't ever have that,' instead of the situational 'No, you can't have that right now.' I'd be upset, too, if I felt that way."

Nate had wandered into the living room. His eyes were red and watery, and his shoes and socks were nowhere in sight. He was standing on his tiptoes, a specific trait of autism.

"We self-calmed in his room today!" the other therapist said, just as Michele set out another plastic bowl for Nate (his fourth meal of the day). Since it was just about noon, the two therapists began packing for the door.

What this meant was that there were two fewer people in the house to lasso Nate if need be. A few minutes after they both departed, the same wave of anxiety I feel standing in the volunteer chute at events flooded my mind, made worse when Michele asked me to watch Nate for "just a second" while she stepped in the other room to call the health insurance company. My main focus was on the door behind him, which led to the garage. Nate had ripped the door open on several previous occasions, and because Michele couldn't risk him wandering into the street, she had an extra deadbolt installed high on the door. (My secondary focus was to ensure he didn't open the front door, either.)

Nate sat still and continued eating.

"Hey Nate, how's your food?" I said, trying to strike up a conversation.

Nate looked at the ceiling.

"Is it good? What are you eating?" I asked.

He popped up and off the chair, and I stood up from the couch. Standing on his tiptoes, he looked into the kitchen, which was an immediate warning sign. I'd been around Nate enough to know that he loves food, but given his digestive problems his intake is carefully monitored. Even a single bite of gluten can set off a chain of boisterous behavior.

Like a transmission kicking into gear, Nate suddenly bolted for the refrigerator, trying to open the door. I closed it behind him and softly said, "No Nate, you've already eaten."

The same happened with the pantry door, and when I denied him as Michele had instructed, he moaned painfully. He tiptoed his way back to the table, grabbed the bowl (which still looked to be half-full) and turned back towards me.

"What is it, Nate?" I asked him. "You want more food? Or are you done?"

He took one step forward, extending the bowl towards me but refusing to make eye contact. I backpedaled rapidly into the kitchen until my back was touching the sink. Nate followed me in, and placed the bowl on the counter.

"Good job, Nate!" I said. "That's awesome!"

"What's awesome?" said Michele as she walked in.

I pointed. "Look! The bowl! He did it himself!"

She smiled widely and said, "Good job, Nate! You want to go to the beach?"

If you find yourself riding to the beach with a mother and her child on the autism spectrum, know there's a good chance you're going to have to sit in the backseat—that way, you can be of assistance in case of an emergency. When Nate's older brother Daniel strapped him into the car seat beside me, he seemed to only gain more energy, squirming and fighting against the restraint.

When we arrived at the beach park, I tried to open my door, but it jammed. I tried again and again, but it wouldn't budge. Finally Michele noticed and said, "Oh, I'm sorry. I have the child lock on. Back in the summer, Nate opened the car door when we were driving even though the child lock was on. We had to get it fixed after that."

Michele walked around the car, opened my door and then unbuckled Nate from his car seat, an action that produced more "oohs."

A white and blue expanse unfolded before us: blue water, blue sky, blue beach umbrellas, and Nate's blue eyes, all set against the white sand poetically dancing in the warm February wind. We were a few miles north of the Deerfield Beach Pier.

As we neared the waterline, Michele allowed Nate to freely run his own circuit, dashing back and forth from the water to dry sand. After a while, Michele instructed us to corral him so that he wouldn't run out of sight—which meant both of us holding an arm and marching our way down the endless beach, only stopping for Michele to inspect seashells. It was so quiet and so peaceful; the sea looked angry, at first, but it was beautiful all the same.

Just as my gaze threatened to get lost in all the blue, my attention was snapped back to Nate. He wouldn't stop yanking at our grip, as he danced with his feet in the tide, kicking up water and getting us soaked. He knew it, too; he cheered, made noises and kept trying to wave his hands in dance, but our grip kept him from doing so. My forearm was already aching and sore as his pulls grew harder and harder.

At this point, we were about 50 yards down the beach. We walked past a group of children that looked to be Nate's age who were building a sandcastle, but Nate didn't notice them. Instead, his gaze seemed fixated on a flock of seagulls ahead.

That's when Michele let go of his arm to inspect a seashell for her collection back home. Nate, realizing that the only thing keeping him from having free reign was my grip, pulled and pulled and pulled and started making noises repeatedly.

"Cccccccccccccccc, Sssssssssssssss" he said, yanking and pulling. I could feel his pulse quickening, even as my grip tightened. Michele, meanwhile, continued to inspect the seashells.

"Caaaaaaaaaaaa, Sssssssssssssss!"

"Caaaaaaa, Sssssssssssssss!"

"Caaaaaaaaaaasssssssss, Sssssstttt!"

"Caaaaaaasssss, Ssssssttttttoooo!"

"Casssssssssssssh, Stoooooooo!"

Suddenly, I heard it: "Casssssssssshhhhhhh, stttttttttopppppppppppp!" he said, pulling with all his might.

"Michele! Michele! Did you just hear what Nate said?" I asked excitedly as the wind whipped tears in my eyes.

She looked up from her shells. "No, what?"

"He said, 'Cash, stop!' Because I was holding him back, he said it! Michele, he knows my name! He knows my name!"

Michele smiled and tossed a seashell back into the sea. "Of course he does. Why wouldn't he?"

Months later, it was 8 a.m. at the second stop on the 2015 Surf Tour: Jupiter, Florida, a quiet beach town just under an hour north of Deerfield Beach. From the parking lot, it was evident the event would include more of what Don Ryan calls the "core surf community"—men with longer hair and tan skin, and attractive, bikini clad girls carrying surfboards, were all headed towards the volunteer sign-up tent.

Jupiter is the southernmost city in Florida that sees the most high-quality swell on a consistent basis. Most of Florida's Atlantic coast sees swell from disturbances and storms, but this isn't really the case as you head south of Jupiter in cities like Deerfield Beach. Why? Well, one perk of living in the next city due south of Jupiter, West Palm Beach, is that the Grand Bahamas are just 50–60 miles directly east. This equates to cheap weekend getaways for fishermen and burned out nine-to-fivers. The downside is that the landmass eats up much of the swell that would otherwise hit its northern counterparts, like Jupiter. Sometimes, swell does filter through, depending on the direction it takes; but even then, the waves aren't of the quality that surfers typically look for.

But if you happen to be a surfer living in South Florida, there's hope—in the form of swirling, white masses with eyes. Depending on the season, hurricanes can push swells into these wave-starved areas. Hurricane Sandy in 2012, for example, gave the South Florida locations life, pumping in triple overhead waves (about three times a person's full height), and wreaking havoc on the area's wooden piers.

But for much of the year, surfers who live in South Florida rack up high mileage from driving to northern Florida locations—Jupiter or further north.

Following the crowd from the parking lot towards the event site, I spied a familiar face walking in my direction. The sun was shining off his wet forehead. He wore crew socks, pecs showing under his white t-shirt. He was grinning from ear to ear, too: it was Keith Arnold, the man who often helped the imposing Byron take on larger participants.

I greeted him with a, "Hey there, Keith! How're you and Christopher doing?" I planned to spend a future event with the family to learn how surfing had become such an integral part of their lives.

"We're great!" he replied. "Last week we went to the Miami Marlins baseball stadium. Christopher got to meet a few players in the dugout and on the field. It was something his special-needs baseball league did."

"The Grand Canyon, Colorado, now this…what has Christopher *not* done?" I said, remembering previous conversations about the family's incredible adventures.

Keith laughed and wiped his forehead. "Well, we try and keep active."

"Are you volunteering?" I asked.

"Yeah, I'll be with Byron again; we teamed up in Deerfield."

"That's right," I said. "Amazing to think that was only two weeks ago. I'll see you out there. I'm sure Michele Weppner will try and get you guys to take Nate out."

Keith responded with an "Okay, great!" and was off in the other direction.

Continuing towards the boardwalk, I noticed a few beachgoers congregating around the large trailer attached to Alfie Fuentes' green Ford Excursion, which houses all of the surfboards and other equipment.

A collage of memories decorates this trailer: photos of Monica riding a four-wheeler in the early morning hours at an event; of Don bear-hugging a participant; a mother standing near the ocean in tears; the seemingly endless alleyway created by tents at a Deerfield Beach event sometime in the past eight years; Lucas Fuentes raising his left hand in victory after surfing; children finger painting on a fire truck; and a row of surfboards in the cool morning sand.

And on last photo, depicting something Michele had told me about time and time again since we met the previous year—Nate, wearing a bright green shirt, lying on an enormous red board in push-up position on a gentle wave, smiling from ear to ear.

Parallel to Alfie's truck and across the street was Don's corresponding Ford and trailer, decorated with its own litany of memories collected through SFA's history.

Making my way closer to the beach, I saw that the main hub tent, directly in front of the boardwalk, was flanked by a long row of tents to the north and south. Hundreds of families and volunteers were already buzzing around the sand, leaving thousands of footprints.

"Our volunteer meeting will be in ten minutes," Don Ryan said over the mic, "so if you have a green wristband and are volunteering, we need you there."

Spying a cooler refuge for my feet where Don looked to be standing, I high-stepped my way over towards him, wincing as my toes hit hot sand. I was already dripping in sweat. I offered my hand to Don, who smiled, his gray mustache twitching as he went in for the typical Don hug—both arms open, necks touching during the embrace.

"If you take a kid out surfing today, let me know. I want to be on your team," I quipped. His eyes widened behind his sunglasses and he bobbed his head, answering back with, "Ok, yeah, of course! Absolutely!"

A few minutes later, I was regretting my decision not to call ahead and make meeting arrangement with Michele. Now I had to trudge through the tents and hunt the Weppner clan down. I tried calling, but only got her voicemail: "Hello, this is Michele Weppner. Sorry I can't come to the phone right now, but if you leave me a message I'll get back to you. Thank you, and remember: never give up hope."

I planned to spend the event with the family, in hopes of learning more about Nate's diagnosis. And to watch him surf, of course.

Scanning each tent for blonde hair, I heard Alfie and the staff ATV coming before I saw him. He slowly drove through the sand with Oliver and Lucas riding on the back, squinting around with an early-morning look.

"Cash!" I heard someone call. I turned to see Michele coming up to me.

"There you are," she said. "We're setting up right here. Want to help me with the beach tent?"

I nodded. "Michele, what time was Nate up this morning?" I inquired. "Was he up early because he knew he was going to surf today?"

"5 a.m.," she said. "He hasn't been sleeping well; I think we had a full moon this week."

Daniel, only 14 years old but already standing at least 5'10", had a tight grip on Nate's wrist. Nate stood on his tiptoes, moaning. "Ooooooooooooh, aaaaaaaaaaah, geeeeeeee!" His eyes zipped back and forth, but his body looked tired.

I was about to learn just how deceiving looks could be. As we began setting the tent up, Nate suddenly wrestled out of Daniel's grip, flashed right in front of me, and was off, a streak of blonde against the sand.

"Daniel, get him!" Michele screamed, fearful of Nate running back onto the boardwalk and near traffic.

Guilt swirled in my stomach as Daniel sped off, leaving a cloud of kicked-up sand in his wake. I'd let my guard down—a luxury I could not afford while Nate was around.

By the time the first session was in the water, I noticed a dilemma: the tide. There looked to be a waist-high swell in the baby blue water, and it crashed onto a sandbar about 20 or 30 yards from shore. The tide was sitting low and, because there was less water above the sandbar, the swell was hitting and pushing it up and over, creating decent waves.

But when high tide would fill in later that afternoon, there was a good chance that the wave wouldn't be breaking. The other option, the shore break, consistently rose up and crashed quickly, creating a thunderous, uninviting pounding.

After living in Florida for a few years, I knew that just because there's a wave in the sea doesn't mean it is surf-able. The difference is as wide as the autism spectrum.

A closeout wave is something you typically don't want to surf, because by the time you paddle out and pop up to a stand, the entire wave of energy has crumbled into whitewash, and there's nowhere to go but straight towards shore. This sort of wave also requires a rapid pop up. But if the wave breaks section by section instead of closing out, a surfer can navigate to a clean area of the wave. That's when maneuvers like airs and turns come into play.

Because the shore break looked tricky, the best bet was the outside break. Don, Kim, Laura, Alfie and the rest of the staff had examined swell predictions for weeks in advance. Of course, there's always an element of uncertainty with surf conditions; but on event day, the trucks were present, the tents were unloaded, and reggae music was already vibing. There were hundreds of people on the beach, many of whom drove for hours just for the event. So there was really no choice but to go in.

"Hey Cash, are you with us for this session? We got Nate!" Byron asked when I made my way down to the waterline. He and Keith had already taken out a participant in the first session.

I nodded, interested to see Byron's techniques—the skills of a tenured master surf instructor.

"How was the first session?" I asked the pair.

Keith laughed, dripping with saltwater. After he caught his breath, he said, "I got knocked on my rear end with the current."

Byron looked as if he was about to respond, but Nate appeared and captured his attention.

"Hey Nate, hop on, brotha'! We're gonna paddle you out," he called.

He picked up Nate as if he weighed nothing, plopped him on the board sitting in the water, jumped on the back of the board and began to paddle.

I followed Keith and another volunteer into the water, and I noticed a certain difficulty shortly after the coolness hit me. None of us could touch the bottom even five yards off the shore. Keith elected to stay near the sand to catch, while another volunteer and I began stroking and sculling as we followed in the board's wake.

About 15 yards off the beach, I reached the volunteer and participant duo. Nate was staring off into the distance, lying firm on his belly with his blonde hair wet and his small arms twitching. He looked energized by all the blue.

"I want to surf him in," Byron said, "but we're gonna play around with it. Hey, Nate, you have a good day, bro?"

Staring at the incoming sets, Byron suddenly flipped the board around and began to paddle into a wave. As one wave drew closer, the other volunteer and I gave the board an extra push.

The duo shot forward. As I treaded water from behind the wave, I could hear Byron bellowing, "Up, Up, Up, Nate!" as they took the wave towards Keith and a packed crowd of onlookers.

While waiting for the duo to paddle back, I was curious if Nate stood or stayed on his belly. I gazed towards the pier, and then at the SFA arena, with volunteers and participants spread throughout the blue expanse. After a few more waves passed, Byron's voice filled the air as he paddled back out.

"Did you guys see that?" he asked, trying to catch his breath. "Nate bailed perfectly, right before we got near the shore. I was about to grab him off so we didn't hit sand, but he's smarter than me…" Nate was smiling and making noises. Even as he was speaking to us, Byron's eyes were fixed on the incoming swell behind us. Moments later, he said, "Hey, help me turn the board around, quick, quick! I see another wave coming…turn, turn, turn!"

The volunteer and I helped Byron maneuver the massive board 180 degrees. He started paddling and again, we helped push. They took the crashing wave in, and I stared at the back of the wave. Moments later the two paddled back, Byron's camouflage hat now missing in action. He didn't seem to notice.

After Nate sang a melody of oohs and ahhs, I noted, "It's gonna be dead high tide soon."

"Yeah, we'll have to see what happens," Bryon replied, his eyes trained on the incoming waves while keeping a hand on Nate so that he didn't spill into the drink. "Here comes another! Get ready to…push!"

Which is exactly what we did, and yet again, the two were accelerating towards the shore thanks to the power of the ocean. It struck me how, throughout the 15-minute session, Byron wasted no time—he seemed to spend more time riding waves than waiting for them. Which in turn meant Nate had little time to let his mind wander into the depths of nervousness or fear, a path which could in turn lead to an outburst. After noting this technique of keeping the participant busy,

I shifted my gaze to Byron and Nate paddling back out. This played on repeat until the horn sounded, and it took minutes for us to make the swim back.

Just as I made it to shore, I heard Byron talking with Michele and Keith. "There are days when Nate can hear me, you know? And some days he can hear me but doesn't listen. I mean, I don't blame him. But today he can hear me. We gotta get him to stand on a board today."

I walked the waterline for the next three sessions following Nate's surf, enthralled in the action as the participants faced their fears by catching waves and playfully wiping out. I also struck up conversations with old friends and met new ones.

When the next session began, after a Laura Fuentes-led lunch break, I ran through the hot sand to snag a water bottle and found Don in mid-conversation, swapping surf stories with another volunteer. I decided to listen in.

"Surfers, we can be 'big headed,'" Don was saying, flashing a smile in my direction. "It takes time to grow out of that. You're moving to Cocoa Beach? One thing you'll learn about living there is that, during big swells, a lot of guys from Orlando are going to come up, and you're going to have to tell them to stay out of the local spots. Because all they're gonna do is not commit. The most perfect set will come, and it'll jack up and one guy will paddle, paddle, paddle, and because of that you won't be able to go, and he'll look down at the wave…and go, 'Uhh, can't do it.' And you'll go, 'Duuude,' and the wave will go unridden! After about the third time this happens, you may start wanting to break people's boards."

Even though Don has experienced this frustration, I can't imagine him ever being confrontational in or out of the water. Since I met Don at the first event years prior, I had never seen anything but joy, happiness and selflessness radiate from Don. He was always someone you could count on giving you a tight hug, followed by him asking you how you were doing—and genuinely listening to your response.

The volunteer and I sat in silence, waiting for Don to continue.

"Man, Hurricane Bill, 2009," Don reminisced. "I surfed Lori Wilson Park—that's where the event will be next month in Cocoa Beach. You could have driven semi-trucks through the barrels—dry. *Dry.*"

Our eyes widened.

"Yeah, that big," Don continued. His grin was from ear to ear. "So I showed up to the beach with a 5'8" quad. And I'm saying to myself, 'Don...you're never gonna stick this.' So I went back to the truck and put the best fins I had in the board.

"That's one of the days the Orlando kids came out. I took my last wave in; it was a dry barrel that turned into shore pound, and man, I just took one for the team. I got covered up but wiped out on the beach. When I got on the beach there were 200 people just standing there, no one paddling out. I said, 'What is going on here? Is this the Twilight Zone?'"

"Because it was so big?" the volunteer guessed.

"Oh yeah," he answered.

"Yeah, I know how that goes," said the volunteer. "I had a girlfriend who wanted to go out surfing with me recently. It was kinda big, and I was kind of scared for her. But she wanted to go."

Don sat up in his chair. "Did she go out?" he asked. "Did she make it out? Because *that's* how we learn how to surf, man. If someone wants to learn, you say, 'Meet me out there.' Anywhere you go, when you're learning, the guys will say, 'Okay, we'll give you tips. But you gotta meet us out there first. I can't help you get out.' You can't navigate that pounding for them."

Florida, and much of the eastern seaboard, is notorious for this "pounding." Florida's waves are known as "beach breaks," named for the way they break atop the shallow sandy bottom. Because this shallow sandy bottom stretches the length of the beach, the only way to paddle out is through the incoming waves, which is what Don was referring to. If beginner surfers aren't familiar with duck diving—a technique that involves pushing the board and its rider under a wave to avoid the brunt of its powerful force—they will struggle to reach the lineup, receiving a lashing in the process. This may even deter them from continuing to paddle out, and they'll instead retreat back to the beach. (This is a contrast to reef breaks, where surfers can paddle through channels created by a lack of reef and arrive in the lineup with a dry head of hair, before paddling towards the reef where the wave is breaking.)

I could have listened to Don tell stories all day, but just then a family appeared to greet and thank him, so with a bottle of water in hand, I started scanning the waterline and noticed a bright yellow flag the same color as Nate's wristband: his session was in the water.

I found him near the sea, with Byron already holding him. "I'll take him by myself," he said, noting that I could stay at the shoreline and catch Nate and the board if need be. "Worst case, me and Nate can just chill out there."

And that's exactly what they did for the entire heat. With conditions diminishing due to the shifting tides, there was no pattern in the water, and the wind had picked up, chopping up the morning's swell lines.

Suddenly, Don's projected voice pierced through the whipping wind. "I want everyone to meet this boy I've been talking to," he announced over the loudspeaker, his voice replacing the reggae music.

This was a common occurrence, a sort of "Meet the Participant" segment that Don would randomly put on. The loud beach grew quiet.

Their conversation went like this:

"So, what's your name?"

A breathy voice answered, "Dylan."

"Dylan, tell us, how old are you?"

"Eight."

"What are you doing today?"

"I came here to surf."

"Nice! How many times have you been in the water today?"

"Umm, three times."

"Did you catch waves?"

"Yes."

"Did you stand up?"

"Well, I was on my knees."

"That makes you a surfer and a ripper," Don declared. "Let's give it up for Dylan, everybody—another one of our participants!" With that, Dylan had the entire beach clapping and cheering for him. It reminded me of something Don had once said to me—that the goal of these events was "to make the participants feel like rock stars."

Judging from Dylan's excited look, today's event was already a success.

Reggae returned to the loudspeakers, and Michele and I watched as Byron continued his attempts to get Nate to stand while struggling to find a wave to paddle into. After a while, Byron let Nate slip off the board and begin to swim around it, within reach of Byron's arms. Nate showcased a huge smile.

"I have a question for you, Michele," I said over the volume of the music, the wind and the beach cheering sections.

"Shoot."

"When I was at your house, I remember you saying something briefly about the divorce rate among parents who have children with special needs. You said there was a large number of divorces, but I didn't hear the rest."

"It's 85 percent," she replied. "You know that my husband Chris and I went through some rough patches. A few years ago, I told him to leave and he wouldn't. I may have said this before, but autism is like a wheel of fortune. It really is; it's the wheel of autism. You don't know if Nate's going to be happy or sad when he wakes up.

"When you first get that diagnosis, you're in shock. The first year we dove straight in; we started ABA, changed his diet…"

She paused, turning to look at the far-off screech of a participant panicking near the chute.

"The second year," she resumed, "we're still doing it. The third year…well, I got pissed off. Fourth year, you realize this isn't going away. Chris started getting pissed off, too. See, when you're pregnant you have these dreams and hopes and ideas of what that baby is going to bring you. Of course, Nate's brought us joy every day. But when you get that label and that diagnosis, you go through the stages of grief all the same. I know that Chris was really mad at the situation, and after a while I told him just to go.

"And he said, 'No. I'm not leaving my kids.' And he didn't. We still have our moments, like when Nate gets up at night."

She paused again, her eyes glued to Nate continuing to gleefully swim around Byron and the surfboard.

"It'll happen sometimes. He tends to wake us up on nights that we do go out. We went out for the Kentucky Derby a few weeks ago. We won $100 that night; it was exciting! But when we got back, he was awake, and in a nasty mood. He was up all night, so I was up all night. My husband works so much, so I take that role on—taking care of Nate. But then I get tired. So yeah, the divorce rate is high, but we… we couldn't *afford* a divorce. I don't see how anyone does it."

I continued to listen, my gaze shifting back and forth from her to Nate in the water.

"It's a continual choice. You wake up every day and choose to keep going—you choose to stay. And that's what I tell Chris: I just say let's take one day at a time."

"Something that I've noticed, being at events, is that there seem to be a lot of single mothers," I observed. "And it breaks my heart."

"Oh yeah," Michele agreed. "I have no idea how they do it. Like I said, we could never afford it. I'd have to go to work; how would I take Nate to school 40 minutes away every morning? What would I do in the summer time? Someone needs to be home when a therapist is there."

The horn sounded, cutting our conversation short.

Scooping up both the board and Nate, Byron paddled in. Once they hit the beach, he released his grip on Nate, who suddenly bolted in the opposite direction.

By the time Michele could get out, "Cash! Grab him!" I already had my arms wrapped around the ten-year-old. "I'm getting better at this," I said, high with adrenaline. Michele nodded in agreement and smiled.

Byron disappeared to place the surfboard near the others, and Chris and Daniel led Nate back to the family tent. I turned to examine the arena opposite the big mess of salt and foam. The beach looked even more crowded now, with the normal Saturday afternoon crowd strolling through the event site.

Continuing my quest to understand autism more, I asked Michele, "Can I ask you something else?" Even though she was still technically a stranger, I felt completely comfortable around her.

It seemed she felt the same. "Of course!" she replied.

"This is because I simply don't know much about autism…but is the future with Nate something you think about frequently? Or is it a 'we'll cross that bridge when we get to it' mentality?"

She didn't hesitate. "Fifty percent of me is in the now, the other half is in future. I have to make my will out very specifically, without any future stocks and bonds. If Nate has any of that, he loses services from the state. I've already thought of guardians for Nate. If Nate had to be in a home, I know some people who would visit him and carry out my wishes. I don't want my kid in one of those places, looking all ragged, but…" Her voice cracked. "These are horrible things we have to consider, that you don't have to do with a typical child. I know Daniel will be fine; he'll be 15 next year. But with Nate, there are so many things."

A pair of arms wrapped around Michele's neck, belonging to Tracy Bastante, whose son Damian was, like Lucas Fuentes, one of the first participants from 2008. The mother-son duo had been traveling with the organization ever since, and because of this, I planned to spend a future event with Tracy and Damian during this year's Surf Tour.

"Hi Tracy. How's Damian doing?" asked Michele.

"He's great!" she quickly answered, pulling her curly dark hair away from her face. "We did a Gnarly Charley surf contest in Deerfield Beach last week."

"How were the waves?" I asked her.

"Small, but perfect for the participants," she answered. "Damian actually caught a wave by himself! He went out, saw a wave coming, paddled for it and popped up."

"Do you think they would let Nate do it?" said Michele.

"Of course they would—good job, Damian!" Tracy erupted. Fifteen yards in front of us was Damian, sliding down the face of a choppy wave and headed straight for shore. His arms were high, with one of his hands forming a shaka (the traditional surfer's sign for hanging loose, a forward-facing fist with thumb and pinkie extended out to the side). As soon as he reached the shore he hopped off the board excitedly.

I was beginning to learn that, while good conversations were taking place on the beach, they would almost always be stopped short by an incredible ride, seeing a familiar face, meeting someone new, or lending a helping hand. From the waves to the surfers, the beach to the music, and everything in-between, there were so many dynamics at play that demanded your attention…and I was loving every bit of it.

"The guy who runs the contests, he makes sure there's a trophy for everyone," Tracy added. "Damian is the only one that cares about first place."

At a minimum, it takes a day or two to process every interaction that happens on the beach during events. The music, the conversations, the surf sessions, the breakthroughs…

After the Jupiter event, all I thought about was Michele and Byron announcing their goal to get Nate to stand on a surfboard. Would it happen this year?

My curiosity then shifted towards surfing as a therapy, as a methodology. Why is it therapeutic? For instance: was there really anything special about the 'Up, Up, Up' saying?

I shared my curiosity with Nate's therapist, hoping her Senior Consultant status would provide insight.

"That phrase often works well when prompting different children to stand up," she explained in an email. "Especially when you change the tone and emphasis in your voice, so that your voice is also going up, up, up, as you say it. It is often said in a tone that combines urgency with both playfulness and firmness, and many children already have experience pairing that phrase with standing up."

I asked if surfing could be therapeutic for Nate, remembering Michele frequently saying that he's much calmer after surf events.

Her response said, "Nate loves the ocean and the beach. When he does Surfers for Autism activities, he is at his favorite place around some of his favorite people. He is able to move toward or away from other people more readily since he is not in a closed environment, such as a house or building.

"Environmental factors play a critical role in learning and performance for many individuals who have autism. This is especially true for

Nate; he is usually happy and relaxed when he is at the beach and in the water and he is able to approach and move away from others, as he can tolerate. One of the most powerful reinforcers that I learned to use with Nate early on in our relationship was to enthusiastically say, 'You are my surfer dude!' He would consistently give me a big smile and great eye contact when I said that to him for coming to me or sitting on request. I think he is more aware and appreciative of surfers and surfing than he can let us know."

4

ADAPTATION

"He came at 27 weeks...and was placed in the Neonatal Intensive Care Unit (NICU). In the middle of that, the doctors thought they were going to lose him because of an infection and so we had a priest baptize him in his incubator. You wouldn't believe how much better he got after we did that."

A daptation is one of the many useful traits that surfing teaches its adherents. Unlike skateboarding, snowboarding, and other sports, the elements underneath one's feet in the sea are unpredictable and can change drastically from one minute to the next.

For example, a change in the tides can reveal the razor-sharp reefs above which the wave breaks; or a change in the wind can turn a sour, windswept session into a glassy dream. Sometimes the predicted swell doesn't arrive; sometimes, when it does, it does so bigger and better up the coast. Other times, the swell is better than ever anticipated. The only consistency with surfing Florida's coast is that it is highly inconsistent. Surfers need to be able to adapt to the demands of the present situation—something which is equally valuable for those who work with children with autism.

Nowhere was this more evident than at the third stop on the 2015 Surf Tour, hosted in Stuart, an equally sleepy beach town like Jupiter, about an hour and a half north of Deerfield Beach. From the parking lot in the morning, the weather looked perfect: quiet and calm (though a bit humid) with a gentle rustling of wind. But after stepping through the boardwalk and out of a thick stand of mangroves, the canvas changed.

Gusting winds, easily 15 to 20 miles per hour, whipped and screamed and howled along the beach. A few steps later, the sea and all its wrath became visible for beachgoers and SFA frequents, a chaotic blue bowl of soup churning without any uniform rhythm in the melody of high winds.

Despite these difficult conditions on that May morning, there was already a group of about 50 sitting in front of Don Ryan, who was speaking into the microphone and bidding a welcome to any newcomers.

Because I'd been to many events before, I split my attention between listening to Don and searching for Keith, Linda, and their son Christopher Arnold who, like the Fuentes and Weppners, were frequent fliers. I had planned on spending the event day learning more about Christopher's diagnosis and the adventures they take him on.

Surveying the scene, I saw Lucas and Oliver Fuentes sitting nearby under the shade of a tent. As I approached, Lucas sat hunched over, laser focused on the family iPad. Oliver spotted me and gave a quick wave.

"Done with school?" I asked.

"We're both done next Thursday!" Oliver said, sweeping his long, curly dark hair out of his eyes and smiling. "What tent are you staying in today?" he asked.

"Well, I'm looking for Christopher's family tent."

"Who?"

"Christopher, you know. Blonde hair, surfs on his belly. Always smiling."

"Oh yeah, yeah! Well, you can stay with us if you want," he offered.

I smiled as I messed up his hair and bid goodbye to Oliver and Lucas, who was still focused on the iPad. Then I was off to continue the search.

Suddenly, a hand shot in the air from another tent a few yards away. It belonged to a frequent flier who I had seen at the previous event: Tracy Bastante. We made small talk for a while, discussing her son Damian, their plans for the summer, and which event would be best for me to spend time with them, until I spotted Linda Arnold walking toward us. Before I could say anything, she provided me with my answer: "We're in the big orange tent over there! The one with the Florida Gators logo."

Then, again beating me to the punch, she continued, "That's where my husband Keith graduated from, not me! Oh gosh, no—I went to Florida State."

Linda is an excited ball of energy, someone who can make the most stoic person burst out laughing. The glass is always half full in her eyes, and she's always ready with actionable wisdom. Smiling, I sidestepped out of the tent, past families and children excitedly buzzing like a hive of bees, to watch Keith complete the tent setup.

"So how many kids are they going to be taking out today during each heat?" I asked. It was looking pretty rough out there.

"Well, usually fifty," Keith said, talking over the wind. "But today I heard they're only doing a few at a time.

"But I would ask Don," he added, unfolding beach chairs. "He would know."

With the volunteer meeting already adjourned, I looked for Don's skinny and rapidly moving figure in the main hub tent. I approached and offered a handshake, but he went in for his trademark full embrace.

Once the proper greetings were over, we both looked out at the sea.

"This is gnarly," he whistled. "Could be our toughest event. Every year, our volunteers have a two-day recovery period after this one. It's like a different ocean here."

He pointed out towards a spot about 20 yards offshore, somewhere in the blue soup's churning and vibrating. "We'll be trying to get to that sandbar, where it's breaking best." Younger participants would stay closer to shore and ride the thundering shore break.

"What's the number on taking kids out today? Less than the usual 50, right?" I asked.

He nodded. "Yeah, 25 at a time. That way we'll have more volunteers per participant—hang on."

As I turned to see what had caught his attention, he was already gone, in hot pursuit after Alfie's ATV, which was on its way back to the trailers for more gear.

While safety was of course the priority, I was interested to see how well the participants would face the unnerving swell, and whether or not this would induce a bigger incidence of breakthroughs or meltdowns. Staring at the chaotic sea made me think that even the average surfer would second guess paddling out today.

It was clear just how difficult the conditions on hand were by the end of the first surfing session. Volunteers were arriving back on the sand, and though they looked tired and were breathing heavily, I heard no complaints. Don was waiting for them, megaphone in hand, looking like a high school football coach trying to cheer his team on after a three-and-out on the football field.

He brought everyone in for a tight huddle, and as I stepped into the circle, I noticed how the group became instantly silent, all eyes focused on Don.

"So, this first session, you either got your legs pulled out from under you and had to fight the current, or you didn't," he began. "The best opportunity is at that sandbar down there. If we all go down there, it *will* be a bit tighter, but I don't want you treading water all day.

Thankfully the tide is receding, so it's getting better. We're not gonna charge the outside; we're gonna do the mid-break. Stay at mid-range.

"We're gonna give you some 9′2″ long boards. If you see a surfboard come in unattended, that means there must be people out there with nothing to float on. Understand? If you lose your board, just forget it. We're gonna have a row of watermen, who will bring you a new one. So if that happens, don't panic; just stay tight and hang on for one minute. It's not that rough, it's just a little bit rippy out there.

"Otherwise, find the shallowest spot and don't be on top of each other. We're going to start our next session, and I don't want any child shorter than this"—he held his hand out to about the level of his chest—"going out there, okay? I need a row of watermen to line up next to me. Way to go guys, way to go!"

I joined everyone in clapping. There was no helping it; the air was suddenly different—electric, motivated, ready.

I scanned the beach crowd and found Linda standing at the waterline with Christopher, who was already walking into the water with a team of volunteers.

His shoulders were low and relaxed, his gait hurried, and he appeared confident—impressively calm in the face of uncertainty. There was no order to the upheaval of water and, within seconds of entering the drink, the ocean had flipped his feet out from under him and everything except his blonde hair disappeared. He quickly bobbed up and the team of volunteers helped put him on the surfboard. Seconds later, he was sprayed and doused with the breaking of whitewash, as they pushed him out to the mid-break sandbar.

Scanning the scene, it was easy to see the magnitude of what a simple marriage between surfing and autism could create. Tens of volunteers were all huddled around boards bearing children with special needs, with many of the participants noticeably fixated on their parents onshore.

Linda shrieked as, directly in front of us, Christopher was already skidding down a wave. Lying on his belly, he careened down the face of the wave with an enormous grin. When the wave suddenly clamped shut in an explosion of white, Chris disappeared in the whitewash for a second, quickly reappearing as his speed increased all the way to shore. Once on dry sand, he started laughing and excitedly walked back into the sea (with the assistance of volunteers) to do it all again.

Linda belted out, "Good job, Christopher!" followed quickly by, "Pull your pants up!"

"What does he like more?" I asked Linda, as the team of volunteers lined Christopher up for another wave. "Surfing? Skiing? Hiking?"

"He likes everything," Linda responded. "Baseball and soccer, too; he goes to those to socialize. I call him my politician."

Surfing provides more for these kids than just an activity to help pass the time and burn off energy. Ask Keith to describe how surfing has been therapeutic for Christopher, and he'll explain that it's increased his coordination, his balance, and his confidence.

In front of us, Christopher was somehow on yet another wave, belly riding down the face as the wave accelerated him through the salty air. He held onto the surfboard as if it were the lap bar of a rollercoaster, beaming the entire time, sliding, sliding…and washing up on the dark sand.

Because of the current, the team was being pushed north as the heat went on, so Linda and I were continuously sidestepping to follow in rhythm. More rides occurred, each with the same outcome—Christopher somehow scoring solid waves, about five seconds long, even in these conditions, and ending on the sand.

After the horn sounded, the team arrived back on the sand and Linda set up to take a photo. The volunteers planted the tail of the board into the sand, holding it vertical as Christopher stood in front. They all formed shakas as Linda excitedly rattled off photo after photo.

"It was a really tough time," Linda matter-of-factly said, handing me a worn photo album with pictures spilling out of the sides.

It was Monday morning—Memorial Day, a week before the third stop on the Surf Tour in Stuart. I sat in the Arnold's living room, wonderfully cozy with two reclining chairs facing the television and a small couch beside the two. Multiple rugs covered the wood floor, and picture frames were draped on the walls throughout the room. Nearly all showed Christopher, revealing that his bleach-blonde hair had been the same bright color for 13 years.

I had been tasked with keeping the Arnold's dog—a black lab named Pepsi—content by keeping a hand on him at all times. Without this comfort, whimpers ensued. But despite this important work, it was the photo album of Christopher, clinging to life after birth, which had my full attention.

"Christopher came at 27 weeks," Linda explained. "He was born on June 9th, and was placed in the Neonatal Intensive Care Unit (NICU). They released him in September. At one point the doctors thought they were going to lose him because of an infection, and so we had a priest…" She paused and reached out to flip a few pages in the album. "We had a priest baptize him in his incubator. You wouldn't believe how much better he got after we did that."

Christopher's official diagnosis was both autism and cerebral palsy. Because he has a lack of muscle tone in his mouth, he was labeled "non-verbal." But the only label that really seemed to fit this 13-year-old boy was that of an adventure-seeking kid, continually smiling, interested in everyone around him. At every Surf Tour afterparty, it's a guarantee that Christopher will approach Don Ryan, wrap his arms around his neck, and try to persuade Don to support his weight.

Suddenly a high-pitched squeal followed by a grunt took my eyes off the photo. It was Christopher, standing at the front door. Keith noticed him waiting, and said, "Christopher is ready; Cash, Linda, are you guys all set? We need to get on the road if we don't want to wait in line at the park."

To get to the Seaquarium, South Florida's glistening sea life arena, visitors must travel to Biscayne Bay, a remnant of Miami, before the Florida Keys and its Seven Mile Bridge come into view. On the way, families zoom through causeways where, right next to the road, beach-goers relax in the baby blue sea, floating, bobbing, and drinking.

Not only did I want to spend more time around Christopher, Keith, and Linda to learn more about how they overcome obstacles; the inner kid in me couldn't turn down a trip to the aquarium.

"This place still looks like something out of the sixties," Keith Arnold said as we swung into the worn-and-weathered parking lot. "Anyone see a handicap spot?"

Keith's description was accurate. The entire structure looked utterly outdated. It seemed like an attraction that Tony Montana would have taken his children to on a Saturday morning.

Throughout the day, what was more intriguing than the splash zones, the dolphins, turtles, and walruses was Christopher's joy at each new sight. Every time a dolphin or a whale would jump, he would flash a big grin and suddenly explode with happiness, which manifested as him biting the neck of his shirt vigorously while he held it near his mouth with both hands. By just the second exhibit, the neck of his shirt looked like it could rip at any moment.

As we stood in line throughout the rest of the day, I continued to learn about the early days of Chris' life.

"After we had Christopher, we decided we weren't going to change our travel lifestyle," Linda said. "There was no way; we liked to go different places and we wanted to take him with us."

At only eight months, Christopher was finally off his oxygen tank and the Arnolds celebrated by taking him to Vail, Colorado that summer, where they introduced him to towering mountains, cool breezes, lush-green forests, and reindeer. He especially liked the reindeer.

During the trip, Keith would strap Christopher to his back and the whole family would hike together. The photographic proof sits in their living room, on the decorative table that Pepsi likes to lie under. And, other than a precautionary stop at a hospital in Denver to make sure his oxygen and breathing levels were holding despite the change in elevation, Christopher did well. He seemed to love being along for the ride.

So they decided to hit the repeat button the following year.

"Have you seen the photo in our house of Christopher sitting on top of a mountain, wearing that blue GAP sweatshirt, with the valley behind him? That was from that year," Keith chimed in. "The next year we went during winter and took him skiing for the first time."

More trips followed, as did repeat visits to Utah—skiing, horseback riding, hiking, even tandem bike rides with Keith and Linda. You name the place, they have a photo of Christopher there—Garden of the Gods, Aspen, rafting on the Eagle River, Pikes Peak.

One of their favorite trips was an eight-day rafting trek through the Grand Canyon. "When he turned eight," Keith recalled, "we spent a week, starting on Memorial Day, on the Colorado River. It was incredible. The whole trip was 277 miles. Our guides had a 37-foot motorized raft and paddles. Every night we'd set up the tent, sleep, and in the morning we would roll everything up, make sure there was no trash and get back in the raft...we saw it all."

These stories absolutely floored me; and what's more, they inspired me. Instead of shrugging their shoulders and saying, "What can we do?" the Arnolds had chosen to combat fear with action. And, in doing so, they had cultivated Christopher's adventurous desires, rather than repressed them. This was the kind of inspiration I couldn't have gleaned if I had simply written a short article about them at an SFA event and moved on.

After we left the park, venturing out through the causeway, the beachgoers, and the Miami traffic, we returned to the family living room where Linda showed me more photos, starting with a photo album from their eight-day rafting trek. Christopher casually sat on the opposite couch and looked to already be excited about the surfing in Stuart planned for the following weekend.

My mouth hung open looking at the photos of Deer Creek Falls, a 150-foot waterfall that empties into a crystal-clear pool surrounded with orange and red rock. Although the noise of the water hitting is supposedly loud, it's the only sound for miles.

A few pages later, there was a photo of the Arnold clan at Havasu Falls, an idyllic oasis where water plunges into a phosphorescent blue pool surrounded by bright red rocks. This presented quite a dilemma for the family, according to Keith: "To get to the falls, you have to swim across a section of the river about 10, maybe 15 yards wide. We knew Christopher couldn't beat the current, so Linda and I decided that we would have to pull him across. We each grabbed a rope at either end and swam it across. I'm not a bad swimmer and I was going as hard as I could, but it still took a while to make progress without being swept down a ways when I crossed. Linda tied her end of the rope onto Christopher, tightly, and I pulled him across."

There were rafting trips too, but Linda didn't get any photos. Instead: "I simply tried to hang onto the raft and Christopher and still take it all in," she said.

During this entire conversation, Christopher sat on the couch and smiled at Pepsi. You'd never imagine that this calm boy was capable of the energetic outbursts I'd seen earlier that day at the Seaquarium.

But Christopher does have his limits—like a plane ride to Mississippi.

"That was terrible," Linda told me. "We were going up there for an augmentative speech camp and we were on this tiny little plane bouncing around in a storm. It was lightning everywhere. He was in the window seat and I had to sit on him—literally! I had to sit on him to keep him from jumping up. He was freaking out, and so was I. We thought they were going to have to turn the plane around because of his anxiety."

Then there was the skiing incident in Park City, Utah. Christopher typically skis with an instructor, who holds a pole horizontal to his body and Christopher's, so they both have something to hold onto as they crisscross down the mountain. On one trip, Christopher somehow evaded the instructor and, perhaps out of curiosity, a sense of daring, or both, turned his skis straight downhill atop one of the main runs. Gravity took control and Christopher rocketed down the mountain.

"I was right there behind him," Keith recalled, "and I was hunched at my knees, skis pointed straight downhill, trying to close in on him. But I couldn't."

The most worrisome part was what lay ahead of Christopher—a ski lift with a crowd of skiers waiting to get on. Keith watched in terror as Christopher sped towards impact, until he plowed into an orange flag that, ironically, was meant to serve as a warning to slow down. An explosion of skis, the color orange, and snow filled the air.

Christopher never said why he turned his skis downhill—given his non-verbal label, he only offered grunts and high-pitched squeals. Keith and Linda may never know why it happened. But what they do know is that it wasn't severe enough to scare him off the slopes. Not long after that, he was back skiing without any hesitation. This innate, daring streak in Christopher helps to explain why he scored some of the best waves of the day in Stuart the following weekend.

Close to lunchtime during the third Tour stop, I spotted a mother at the waterline who I knew well, for reasons that owed a lot to coincidence.

Like the Fuentes, the Weppners, and the Arnolds, Kami Lambert and her daughter Skye are frequent fliers. Their attendance at events is almost religious: rarely do they miss one. Thanks to this dedication, Skye, 14 years old, is one of the more experienced surfers you'll see on event days. Her surfing stands out thanks to her fantastic ability to balance and make the drop regardless of the wave size. Plus, she loves all things eccentric and pink.

Though we share the same last name, Kami and I are not related, something that caused a bit of a riff when I first met Michele and Nate Weppner.

Over a year prior to the Deerfield Beach event, I called Michele to schedule a visit. Upon entering her house, she led me to the backyard, where Nate was running around in typical naked fashion.

After some small talk, Michele looked at me and said, "You're Kami's son, right?"

I froze.

"Kami?" I asked, puzzled.

"Yeah, Kami Lambert," she replied. "She and her daughter Skye… they go to all the events. Skye's a bit older…wait, you're *not* related to them?"

I shrugged. "Actually, no."

She pulled her shoulders back, looked at naked Nate in the pool, then back at me.

"Well, who the hell are you, then?" she asked.

Thankfully she didn't kick me out of the house. To this day, it's something that Kami and I still reminisce about.

"How was your drive down here to Stuart?" I asked Kami, remembering that she and Skye live outside of Cocoa Beach, the next stop on the Surf Tour. Her calm laid-back demeanor was clearly evident in contrast to the controlled mayhem surrounding us.

"Not bad. One hour maybe; Cocoa Beach isn't too far." She looked out at the waterline and the sea.

"Everyone says Stuart is the toughest event," she continued, "and Skye loves the big waves…but man, is it rough. I feel bad for the volunteers. They're gonna be wiped out after this."

I nodded. "You guys are coming to Cocoa Beach, right?" I asked.

She shook her head sadly. "We didn't get into Cocoa Beach, actually. It filled up too quickly. But I told Skye, 'Hey, we're still going to go, right?' And she said, 'Absolutely!' So we signed up as volunteers. It will be her first volunteer experience."

This is another impressive facet of SFA: not only do Skye and the other participants have the opportunity to surf, experiencing its therapeutic benefits and making friends all the while; as they grow older, they are learning the importance of volunteering and helping others, something the Fuentes have been practicing with Miranda and Oliver.

I was relieved to hear Kami and Skye would be at the next event on the Tour. I'd planned on hearing their stories of diagnosis and breakthroughs in Cocoa, a location known for its illustrious history and solid surf.

Kami and I continued our conversation until we reached the waterline, where the first person we saw was Byron, breathing heavily and carrying a board.

"So low tide is at noon, yeah?" I asked him.

"Yeah man, it's gonna be brutal," he replied. "Low tide gets nasty… just pitching right on that sandbar."

"Can you stand out there well?"

"It depends where you're at, man. I found an oasis of sand bar and just rode shotgun with some kids. Short rides, you know; but fast. *Fast*, fast." His gaze moved to a bit behind me. "Oh hey, there's Nate!"

In less than a minute, Byron had Nate in one arm and a surfboard in the other as he charged back into the sea. Michele came up to stand beside us.

"Where's Chris?" I asked her, noticing her husband was absent.

"Volunteering today," she replied, before cheering, "Look at Evan! Go, Evan!"

Directly in front of us, Byron was holding the board steady for Nate at the mid-break. Beside him was Evan, the son of Christine Poe—yet another SFA frequent flier who I'd be shadowing at a future event—on a wave, pulling his knees to his chest and rising. Just as the board began to wobble in the whitewash, he crouched and sprang off.

"Good job, Evan!" his mother cheered, rattling off photos on her phone. Evan is just one of her boys: she also has Ethan, Evan's twin brother, both of whom have autism and participate in as many SFA events as possible.

This is why watching participants surf can leave the crowd almost as exhausted as their children: not only are you constantly seeing familiar faces and meeting new friends, you're likely to be cheering for multiple participants at the same time as they ride on the same wave. Splitting your attention during that kind of emotional high can wipe you out.

Michele suddenly exploded: "THERE HE GOES! GO, NATE!"

Byron pushed Nate on a wave and despite the "Up, Nate, Up, Up!" from both Byron and Michele, Nate continued to lay contently on his belly and slid into the sand, with Byron hot in pursuit.

Nate sliding towards us on his belly on the next wave kicked Michele into high gear, and she continued yelling, "NATE, NATE, NATE! UP, UP, UP! Oh, he's trying!"

Minutes later, the session ended and, after photos with the volunteers, the two blonde frequent fliers and their kin went their separate ways. I began to look forward to spending time with Christine Poe and her twin boys at a future event, to better understand what it's like to face a double dose of autism.

The horn sounded again, signaling the start of the next heat, as Linda hurriedly got Christopher ready for his session.

I followed the two toward the waterline, when I saw Don drive by on an ATV. Something about it caught my attention, and when I spotted Miranda Fuentes near the volunteer chute, I decided to ask her about it: "Question!"

She squinted and smiled, her snow-white teeth visible. "Yessssssss?"

"So, there's a rainbow spinning wheel taped to the handlebar on one of the ATVs," I said with a laugh. "Just saw Don with it—what's the story behind that? Seems kind of odd for big men with big trucks to have this colorful, spinning wheel..."

She smiled. "Oh, a kid came up one day and left it there for Don. He decided to keep it. Don't you think it adds a good touch?"

Before I could respond, she was handed a participant and she disappeared in the direction of the sea with a board in tow.

"So Keith has been volunteering all day?" I asked Linda, who was standing a few feet away with eyes on Christopher in the water.

"Yes, he has. He loves doing it, you know," she replied. She watched her son for a few moments, before confiding, "This week, Christopher just learned how to eat an apple."

I stayed quiet, knowing she'd explain. "You know, because he lacks muscle tone in his mouth," she continued. "Think about how much you use your tongue when you chew—he can't do that. So we've been working on that."

In front of us, Christopher was pushed onto a wave by a team of volunteers. The board slid sideways and he rolled off, slamming into the chaotic drink before being immediately pulled up by a volunteer.

"Does he ever get frustrated by not being able to communicate?" I asked.

"Oh, all the time," she said. "Especially in restaurants, where it's hard for me to figure out what he wants. He's almost flipped tables before. That's why we use a device where you press icons and it speaks for you. We got it through the school."

I couldn't begin to image that frustration—wanting so badly to use your voice, but simply not being able to.

"That said, there's something about church with Christopher. Really, he's a saint in Mass. He knows when to sit, when to stand, when to kneel. He never likes missing a Sunday, either. After church he always has to say 'hello' to the priest and to everyone in the congregation with a hug." She smiled. "He's my little politician."

The rest of the day of surfing and other beach activities became a blur; lunch was followed by heat after heat as Keith and I took Christopher out into the sea. When my feet did touch sand in the water, it was difficult to get any kind of grip because of the river-like current.

By the afternoon, the waves were unorganized pulses of chop. When we finally had a wave push through looking the right size, we'd push Christopher on it only for the ball of energy to dissipate. And there was Christopher on his belly, grinning, right in the middle of the impact zone.

So we'd scoop both him and the board up, receiving a few white-water lashes in the process, and continue trying.

But other than a few short rides, conditions had deteriorated and the rest of the session played out without any rides quite as good as the very first session. But this didn't seem to matter to Christopher; once we waded to the shore, he was beaming as usual during Linda's photo session, with each photo destined to end up in the overflowing picture frames in their living room.

With the last heat of the event wrapping up in the water, I ventured back to the Arnold family tent to gather my belongings, saying good-bye to several families—including the Fuentes, Weppners, Tracy and Damian, Kami and Skye and the Poes—along the way. My sandy feet hit the boardwalk and a few minutes later, behind the protection of the mangroves, the wind disappeared and it was suddenly quiet. Dodging other families packing their vehicles, I realized just how incredible the parents were today to not only brave the high winds throughout the day, but to entrust their children to volunteers in the chaotic sea. In turn, these volunteers showcased incredible adaptation by battling the conditions and their own exhaustion all so that the participants have an opportunity for therapeutic experiences. I didn't expect to see this kind of love and sacrifice; it was an undercurrent—more powerful than the current at Stuart—that I had never imagined.

Already, I found myself anticipating the breakthroughs and powerful stories that surely awaited me at future stops on the Surf Tour.

5
THE ORIGINS OF SFA

"One in 57 boys have autism. Either way, it's tough to swallow and very alarming. If we don't dedicate however many scientists it takes to figure out what's causing this, we're in trouble. Look at it this way: in 20 years, these children will be young adults, and many will continue to need full time care. What are we going to do then?"

In the weeks between the Stuart event and the event to follow (Cocoa Beach), I took some time to dig through my personal SFA archive. Nearly all SFA participants keep some form of record—usually in the form of photos that show their child's progress and growth through year after year of surfing. Some even have press clippings of their child being featured in newspapers and magazines. My archive, which dates back just over half a decade, consists of articles covering SFA events written for different publications.

This search was fueled by a desire to "relive" the origins of SFA, as seen through the eyes of co-founder Don Ryan, whom I've had the opportunity to interview multiple times.

The first time I interviewed Don Ryan, we were sitting on a wooden walkway spanning 50 yards to the beach in Jacksonville Beach. This alone was an honor and a victory, because when I'd tried to pry him away earlier for quotes, he'd taken one look at me, smiled, and agreed, but quickly explained it would have to wait. His responsibilities at the event, which were considerable, included helping with the event's mechanics, meeting and greeting families, cheering on the waterline, and more.

So when he *did* find the time, I felt the need to be brief and make every question count. The wind was whipping around our figures, and I was a bit worried that my recorder wouldn't pick up his voice; after all, there was no way I would be able to replicate or paraphrase his words—they were simply too good.

In my journalism career, I've interviewed a host of high-profile individuals, spanning from NFL players (I worked as a member of the Gameday Media Relations staff for the Miami Dolphins, helping with post-game interviews in the locker rooms); America's most iconic fishermen and hunters (while reporting for ESPN Outdoors and the Outdoor Channel); and even the world's top surfers (serving as the editor of Hawaii's Freesurf Magazine).

But none of these experiences was as memorable as my interviews with Don Ryan. There's something about "the Don" that makes him more than just a leader worth following: each sentence he speaks carries power and wisdom. It was almost as if he was speaking a different language entirely, and I found myself wanting to become bilingual.

His name couldn't be more fitting, because from that moment forward, every time I was around the man I wanted to sit and listen—listen to the Don, an Italian honorific referring to his role as the brain, the leader of a family.

"Surfers for Autism all began with a simple idea," he explained to me with a smile. "Knowing the calming and therapeutic effect of water to individuals with autism spectrum disorder, we thought, why not invite them to the beach? We started planning; being an extremist, I said, 'Let's not only take these kids surfing—let's raise some funds, bring some food, give them a concert, and treat them like rock stars.'"

On the beach is where things change for the participants. And, perhaps unsurprisingly, for the volunteers as well. "To bind an entire community to something so simple and to have such a profound impact on kids on the spectrum was amazing," Don said. "And so it began."

But it wasn't all as easy or straightforward as he made it sound. While the green SFA crew was excited, there was also plenty of anxiety. "We had totally committed to a lot of unknowns and it was upon us, no turning back. In the back of your mind you are wondering if anyone will show up. And what do we do if they do?"

Don said that he knew, deep down, there would be benefits for everyone involved. But he didn't realize the true magnitude. "But at the end of that day, the reality was that I had absolutely no idea of the seemingly immeasurable impact this would have—not only for the kids attending, but for the volunteers and an entire community. I personally was changed forever."

Just as the families and volunteers each have emotional, powerful stories following their first event, Don does as well. "I witnessed many breakthroughs on our first day," he said. "I witnessed a child's first words; I witnessed children not receptive to touch, embracing and hand holding; I witnessed individuals with extreme social challenges make friends…and I witnessed parents, siblings, family members and caregivers cry with joy over these breakthroughs and stand in disbelief at the capabilities these individuals possess."

Don continued: "For the participants at these events, it's pure overstimulation. A sort of shock and awe. To remove a possibly regimented, withdrawn and/or socially awkward individual from their 'safe' environment and introduce them to so many new things and people all at once may seem incomprehensible or radical, but the results speak for themselves. Just ask the parent of a nonverbal child who just spoke to them for the first time. For the volunteer, it's the opportunity to have a genuine positive impact and realistically change the lives of hundreds of people for the better in just one afternoon."

The year after our first interview in Jacksonville Beach, I pitched an idea to *Eastern Surf Magazine*, a publication that covers all things surfing on the Atlantic Coast of the U.S., to cover the Surf Tour stop in Jupiter. The editor consented, and I made the mistake of telling Don beforehand that the story was about him. He quickly and sternly made it known that SFA was not, and never will be, about himself.

He then mysteriously told me to meet him and the SFA crew in a little beach town north of Jupiter called Stuart, for "a special event at the courthouse." So the next day I skipped one of my college journalism classes, and soon found myself sitting inside a small courtroom filled with about 20 chairs, all facing an expansive wooden desk.

Seated behind the desk were people who were clearly of authority. The air was quiet and stiff, and half the chairs were filled with clean-shaven men in dress trousers and ties.

Moments before the meeting began, the door blew open and energy, color and excitement injected itself into the room in the form of the SFA entourage, led by Don and Kim Ryan. Don was dressed in a blue button up and khaki pants, with others sporting board shorts and SFA t-shirts.

Things began to make sense when Don was called in front of the assembly to receive an award from the mayor, who declared May 12th as "Surfers for Autism Day." Don's cheering section was boisterous and in full form that day.

Afterwards, I followed Don's roaring F-250 (festooned with SFA bumper stickers) to the quiet downtown district in Stuart for a congratulatory meal. A table for 15 or so was set before us. Don (sporting a black SFA hat) and I sat at an opposite table with my laptop opened, where I typed away at every word he said. With every answer he provided, he looked directly into my eyes.

In all my life, this was the only time I've ever seen a grown man passionately tear up about a cause, simply by discussing it with someone who was essentially a stranger.

As I wrote in my article, which Eastern Surf Magazine later published: "In-between questions, volunteers congratulated Ryan, to which he'd point at the proclamation and say, "No, congratulations to *you*. Can you believe what we've accomplished?"

After that first event in Deerfield Beach, the SFA workers—Don included—were completely blown away. Initially, the plan was to have an annual event in South Florida. "We didn't know how to react—it was that impactful for the families there. But we decided this was so much bigger than all of us. We realized the potential it had for other communities and other families. It was numbing to see a community come together, bound to one cause—to give children the day of their lives. It was overwhelming—just unbelievable."

The next morning after that first event, Don paddled out on a longboard, but there were no waves to be had; instead of surfing, he watched the sunrise and started crying. "I went through a lot of soul searching, and this idea to help families touched by autism became my mission. I was called and led to it. Ever since that moment, I've answered that call. It would have been irresponsible not to."

There are so many powerful aspects of SFA events, from the community to the friendships, the healthy activities, and more. But through it all, the central focus remains to be the therapeutic aspect to the participants. "Barriers are broken, as far as social and sensory issues," Don told me. "Some kids say their first words to their mother; some kids are high-fiving when they've never touched people before. I've seen some kids carried from the car to a towel on the beach because they don't want to touch the sand, but within four hours, they're burying each other in the sand."

From the first event in 2008 to every event that has come after it, Don says he has seen a profound pattern, regardless of whether it takes 10 minutes to get a child in the water or two to four hours: "Often, a volunteer will get them out in the water as quickly as possible, turn their surfboard around, push them into the first wave, and it's over. I see the same situation every time—the kid's hands come up from squeezing the rail, chest pushed out, arms wide, eyes big...and then the smile comes. At that specific moment, the kid usually looks to the left, to the right, and behind to see that no one is touching them. That's their moment, their wave, their surfboard."

During our interview in 2015, Don mentioned to me that, "One in 57 boys have autism. If we don't dedicate however many scientists it takes to figure out what's causing this, we're in trouble. Look at it this way—in 20 years, these children will be young adults and many will continue to need full time care. What are we going to do then?"

6

DISCOVERING
IDENTITIES

"At one point, she wouldn't respond to us. Your own child,
not responding to your voice..."

lthough every SFA event starts with a volunteer meeting, and
each discusses the same dynamics as the previous events, each one
seems to carry a different tone, one which reflects the attitude and
vibe at the event site.

Deerfield Beach's meeting brimmed with contagious excitement
and pulsing energy. The Jupiter and Stuart meetings also exuded excitement, but those two events seemed more laid back. Now, standing in
arguably the thickest crowd of volunteers yet, Don was handed the
mic, and it was immediately clear that Cocoa Beach was going to be a
high-energy event.

"We are landing a helicopter here today," Don announced in front
of the roughly 400 volunteers sitting in the cool Cocoa Beach morning
sand, where the humidity resembled a sauna.

Though Cocoa Beach is only two hours north of where the Tour
first started, both the scenery and the aesthetic couldn't be more
different. Whereas Deerfield, Jupiter and Stuart feature beaches with

dramatic and calf-burning inclines, the beach at Cocoa Beach looked flat, long, and compact, and far easier to walk through.

And, while all the previous stops on the Tour were indeed beach towns, none of them have as much surfing in their blood as Cocoa Beach. Not only does the East Coast Surfing Hall of Fame sit in the small, Central Florida town; Kelly Slater, the 11-time world surfing champion, calls the area home. There's even an iconic statue of him when driving north into Cocoa.

The popularity of this area seems to hinge on its location. The town sits roughly an hour east of Orlando, with its ever-bustling theme parks, and sees some of the most consistent swell in the state. Few Miami-like high rises exist in Cocoa Beach, and daily life moves at a much slower pace.

"The helicopter landing zone will be on the parking lot in the grass; we're gonna let the kids see it during lunch," Don continued, as the enormous crowd began to applaud.

"We are taking 200 kids in the ocean, and we still have another 300 on the waiting list," Don went on. "So those who can't surf—they'll be coming out for the fun stuff we do today. Behind me in the parking lot you can see some painting fire trucks."

Don went on to break down the guidelines for the day's events, stressing the importance of staying alert and hydrated. "It's hot," he reminded us, "and this is sweltering, record-breaking weather. And I say that as a native. So drink water all day; it's free, and it's endless—we will not run out of water."

Also included in the day's activities was a live painting from Mark Longnecker, who had received TV acclaim for being on the hit show *Ink Masters*. Mark is also known to paint surfboards—splashing bright colors and tropical-themed designs on white foam—and donate them to SFA, who in turn gives the boards away to raffle ticket holders on event day.

A prayer served as the meeting's adjournment, and the crowd began to dissipate throughout the beach. As I looked toward the waterline, peering through the wall of people clad in bikinis and board shorts, I spotted Tracy and her son, Damian, with a newsperson armed with a tripod and camera.

By the time I made my way within earshot, Tracy was already gushing to the camera: "We've been with Surfers for Autism for 8 years. We were at the first event in 2008, and Damian was one of the first ones in the water. Have I seen benefits? Yes; not just for him, but for me also. He's now smiling, happy, much more engaged. SFA events help give him self-confidence and an identity. Now, he even likes to compete in surfing."

Tracy traded places with Damian, who looked down at the sand and began: "This is Damian Richter reporting live from Surfers for Autism…"

As Damian continued, my mind drifted back to the story of Damian's diagnosis that Tracy told me. The story is a microcosm of the raw emotions felt throughout the arduous autism process.

"At 2 years old, we noticed that Damian wasn't progressing in his speech," recalled Tracy. "He said very few words, but always seemed to understand what we said. At one of his checkups, I asked his pediatrician about it, but she told me not worry; that he might just be a late talker.

"Damian did some quirky things, but I thought they were part of his personality. He would flap his hands when he was excited, and he would rock when watching TV or listening to music. Sometimes he would line his toys up; I just thought it was a parade.

"He also liked to spin himself in circles. Once, my sister saw him doing that and said she knew a little boy who would spin like that, and that the boy had autism. I got so mad at her."

So Tracy went back to her pediatrician and boldly asked if her son had autism. The doctor reassured her, saying that Damian was too affectionate and aware of things around him to be considered for autism.

Tracy believed the pediatrician, of course. How could you not, in her position?

Even when someone from the state came to evaluate Damian for speech therapy, the social worker sided with the doctor. It was official: Damian didn't have autism.

But in the months to come, one speech therapist, who observed Damian often, further fueled the emotional rollercoaster by suggesting Tracy should go back—yet again—and see what the tests revealed. "I was heartbroken, but I set an appointment," she said.

That appointment was on April 12, 2005—a day Tracy will never forget.

"After a three hour-long battery of tests and observations, they told us that Damian had mild to moderate autism," she said. "That is when my world changed. All I knew about autism at that point and time was what I had seen in that movie, *Rainman*."

I was already aware of *Rainman*, the 1988 film which saw Tom Cruise discover he had a younger brother with autism, and which chronicled their cross-country road trip as they try to learn more about one another. The film was groundbreaking in the sense that, for the first time, the mainstream was being exposed to a story about someone with autism. But while many in the autism community hoped this film would start the dominoes falling, sparking a flurry of more films to help the public understand more about autism, this didn't happen. Today, while there are a few movies and television shows that address autism, those in the autism community would still like for more to be available to help promote autism awareness.

"When we asked what this diagnosis meant, what the prognosis was, they told us very negative things," Tracy said. "They said he might never talk, never tell us he loves us. He'd never have pretend play or an imagination. I had to stop them, while they were saying all this. I asked them to please, stop telling me what he might not be able to do and start telling us what he *will* be able to do; what we needed to do to help him."

But the doctor's response was equally heartbreaking: "They couldn't tell us what he would be able to do, but that he would need intense therapies," she continued. "We left there devastated and confused. But after a few days of coming to grips with his diagnosis, I remember watching Damian sleep and feeling so much love for him that I became determined to do everything I could to help him. And so began our journey into the world of autism and all the therapies."

"Damian is surfing in the second group today," Tracy said after the cameraman left, the heat of the crowd stifling the air around us. Her tone, like always, was warm and friendly.

"But isn't he always in the first?" I asked.

"Well, I didn't get here fast enough," she exclaimed. "This event fills up as fast at Deerfield! Oh, and I just found out the State Championships for the Special Olympics is here in Cocoa Beach the same weekend of the SFA event later this year in Tybee Island, during September."

"The Championship Special Olympics," Damian repeated, his eyes focused on the sand at his feet. His brown curly hair—like Tracy's—danced in the wind.

Tracy continued, "And I asked him, which one do you want to do? He said either one, but I need for him to pick one."

Tracy followed Damian's line of sight to the sand, noticing her own feet.

"I'm glad they're doing the tattoo party again this year, too," she quickly remarked.

"A tattoo party?" I asked.

"We did it two years ago, and a bunch of us got SFA tattoos, with the proceeds going back to the organization. I did, so did Michele Weppner; Laura Fuentes, too."

Tracy raised her leg, pointing at her ankle.

"See? They did a person with a surfboard, but they didn't put fins on the surfboard. I want them to add the fins this time, but it took me like four hours to get psyched up enough to do it the first time."

As we waited for Damian's heat to enter the water, I couldn't think of any other cause besides Surfers for Autism that could convince a handful of conservative mothers to get tattoos.

"So I'm presuming those two...things? Can I call them things? Are launch pads from the Cape?" I asked Kami Lambert, as we stood watching the first session in the water. After Tracy and Damian had ventured back to their tent, I'd found Kami at the waterline.

Kami nodded to me and smiled, looking like she always does—relaxed, in spite of the energy of the day—and explained how Skye, who wasn't initially planning to surf at this event, had entered after a participant or two ended up canceling.

"So how long have you guys lived around here?" I asked.

"Twenty-five years; we're about 50 minutes south," she said, her attention still drawn towards the sea, where participants were being pushed out into perfect, fun-sized brown rollers. It was a far cry from the conditions in Stuart and Jupiter, and a much larger swell size compared to the conditions seen in Deerfield Beach.

I decided to ask the question that every SFA family has an instant answer to: "What was your first event?"

"Ponce Inlet when Skye was 10," she said. "She's 14 now; that was August 2011. I'd heard about SFA from a friend. Her son and Skye went to school together. So I jumped on Facebook and saw the photos of people surfing and immediately wanted to go."

"Many of the families I've spoken to jumped right into attending as many events as they could after that, instead of slowly attending more and more. Was that the case for you guys as well?"

"At Ponce Inlet, we fell in love and did three events: Ponce, St. Augustine, and Jacksonville Beach," she answered. "During the Jacksonville event, Skye actually got lost. Don said something on the microphone—that the weather could get bad, and that we needed to get off the beach. So Skye hightailed it to the bathrooms at the hotel; she is mortified of storms. Don ended up blowing the lost-child siren until someone found her in the bathroom...but anyways, at her first event, she stood up."

"During the first session?" I asked.

"The very first wave!" she excitedly replied. "She's always been a water bug. She does gymnastics and that's helped with her balance. We used gymnastics as an occupational therapy type of thing."

"So what was the diagnosis like?" I asked, fighting to be heard above the roar of volunteers and families cheering for surfers. "Was it a doctor who initially gave you the diagnosis, or did you notice something that set off alarms?"

"It was actually my mom who said something to me," she recalled. "She was concerned because Skye wasn't answering to her name. Not only that, she would spin bowls around and around, take puzzles apart and put them back together, turn them upside down and put them together. She would page through books over and over again. I thought that was typical at first, but as time wore on...it was the extent to which she was doing these things. I mean, for hours.

"She went to occupational therapy twice a week and we had a speech therapist come twice a week to improve the muscle tone and sensory issues in in her mouth. One of the best things we did was the Verbal ABA (Applied Behavior Analysis) therapy. My mom would take her from therapy to therapy so that my husband and I could continue working. Plus, at that time our insurance wouldn't cover anything, including the autism specialist; we had to pay for everything out of our own pocket."

A boy with a dry head of hair caught my attention as he streaked towards us, riding on a wave. And I wasn't the only one noticing; the beach was absolutely erupting into cheers! Tearing myself away from the sight, I refocused my attention on Kami.

"We ended up getting her on a gluten-free, casein-free diet along with a verbal ABA therapist because she was nonverbal. From age two, she ran around the house singing "Ma-mama-mama-mama-mama," perfectly to the tune of Mozart's *Eine Kleine Nachtmusik*. Though it was amazing, it wasn't meaningful; but because of her excellent ABA therapist, by about three and a half, she began saying words. Now she's totally mainstreamed. But it took lots of hard work and lots of wonderful people."

Throughout my time with SFA, I'd picked up most of the lingo: by saying that Skye was mainstreamed, Kami meant that she had become integrated into regular school classes.

After we watched a few more participants excitedly ride by on waves, I replied, "It's incredible that something Don and others birthed out of simply giving kids a day at the beach can be so influential. Skye seems like one of the oldest kids here, and it's a part of her now, forever."

Kami nodded. "The biggest thing Skye has gotten out of SFA is a sense of identity, as a surfer and as family. Because of this love and acceptance, she has gained so much confidence, not just in surfing but in interacting with people. She has no fear; or, if she does, she has the courage and persistence to work through it.

"I'd see her interact with other kids. She's very outgoing, very friendly...but she doesn't get the cues, the social cues. You don't go up to someone that age and shake their hand, and say 'Good morning!' They'll just grunt and roll their eyes. Sometimes I'd get pissed off and want to say, 'Is there anything wrong with a 'Hello' as a response?' But now she's making more and more friends with people she sees at events."

Before I could respond, multiple whistles blew and the whole atmosphere of the beach changed. Don's voice boomed over the microphone repeatedly: "MANDATORY WATER BREAK, EVERYONE. PLEASE GET OUT OF THE WATER! MANDATORY WATER BREAK!" The teams of volunteers rapidly hoisted the smallest children in their arms. Older participants took the next wave into the sand. But instead of anxiety, the general tone was one of confusion.

Confusion for many, but not for all: "Most of us know what 'mandatory water break' means," said Tracy Bastante, smiling. "Don's done this before, like that one time in Stuart."

We were standing at the waterline, and after a brief pause of roasting in the heat (it turned out someone may or may not have seen a shark), the spotters gave the green light to resume surfing. Damian took full advantage by showcasing his skills in the best waves the 2015 Surf Tour had seen up to this point.

He was pushed on a wave and popped up in one fluid motion with ease. A team pushing another participant out towards the lineup came into Damian's sight. The two were heading for impact but Damian quickly stomped on the back pad of the surfboard, shifting direction and veering to the right of oncoming traffic. As if the obstacle was never in his path, he continued gaining speed until he ended the ride on the sand.

"His pop ups seem to be even faster today!" I remarked, before getting into the topic at hand: Damian's surfing talent.

"So Damian loves competition?" I asked. "Can you tell me more?"

"Are you kidding?" she replied. Perhaps influenced by Damian, she was moving full speed into the conversation. "He loves competing! And now I've got him to where he's a good sport even if he doesn't win.

Though at the last three local surf events, the Gnarly Charley's, he won first place."

Out of the blue, Don Ryan streaked in front of us, running parallel to the waterline. He screeched to a halt, his eyes locked on a little girl, who looked to be no older than five or six, riding whitewash. He was beaming as he called her out: "Yeah! Everyone see this? Let's give her a round of applause!" Then, as fast as he'd arrived, he was gone.

Meanwhile, Damian was up and riding again, a flawless pop up into a full stance with his left foot forward and right foot back, hands pointed towards the beach and eyes on the tip of the surfboard.

"How's school going for Damian?" I asked after he completed the wave.

"He's mainstreamed," said Tracy. "The hardest thing is getting him to focus and pay attention. He does good in history; he's great with straight memorization. Remember, I was telling you before, about the dates?"

Instantly, the memory clicked. Over a year ago, I'd spent the afternoon with Damian and Tracy at a public park near their home in Deerfield Beach. While pushing Damian on the swing, Tracy challenged me to ask him the date of any previous SFA event, any place, any year. And so I did. He'd rattled off the specific date for every event I mentioned, sounding completely confident in doing so.

Next to us, I noticed Lucas Fuentes carefully dipping his feet into the cool, brown water. Just behind Lucas, I saw a mother with a death grip on her blonde-headed boy, who wouldn't stop jumping. It was Nate Weppner and his mother, Michele.

Within minutes, Damian's session was out of the water and taking photos while Nate was headed into the water.

"So our insurance company wants to cut back on Nate's therapy," Michele said after we exchanged greetings, and I'd asked her about any new developments. Her full attention was on Nate and his team of two volunteers.

"They know nothing of my son or his therapy," she said. "They want to cut back to ten hours. Even though all the research I've done on this says don't go under 20."

Instead of asking questions, I stayed silent and lent a listening ear.

"We *were* making do with therapy at 15 hours. But I talked to my BCBA—you remember her, right?" She was referring to the Board Certified Behavior Analyst who worked with Nate; I'd met her on one of my previous visits to the Weppner's. "She said that in the next year the company may pull it back to 10. I wrote a letter to the insurance commission and some legislators in Tallahassee because, if they think they're going to dictate to my son what he needs or else drop him, that's not an answer."

If SFA events were my crash course on autism, these conversations were my textbooks. Before this conversation (and others like it, which echoed everything Michele was saying), I would never have realized the incredible struggle and stress that comes from insurance companies only paying for so much, regardless of how much more may be needed.

"They don't understand that if you don't help these kids now, you'll have to help them later. It's bullshit!" She scowled. "Excuse my language, but it really is. Nate had to take a break from therapy when I was dealing with the insurance company a month ago. By the third day he was saying the therapist's name over and over again, because he's so used to it. And meanwhile I'm crying, knowing he won't have it today."

I stayed silent, and just let her get it all out. She wasn't yelling; she was venting what I deemed to be righteous, justified anger. I felt as though she wasn't just speaking on behalf of Nate; she was also speaking for so many others who endure the same struggle.

"It's just been a frustrating three weeks—no school, no therapy," she continued. "UP, UP, UP, NAAAAATE!"

Just like that, her mood completely shifted.

Nate was on a wave and shooting towards us belly first, with a volunteer on the tail of the board. Nate, perhaps because of the volunteer's encouragement or even hearing his mother's cry, popped to his knees, and began to stand on one leg before jumping off the board.

"We're getting there, we're getting closer, dude!" I heard the volunteer say as they came within earshot. The volunteer had a brief wrestle with the board and Nate, before taking the two back into the sea.

"See, before he used to run away when they would get near the beach," Michele remarked. "Did you see how he waited for the volunteer to pick him up? That's ABA."

Then she sighed. "Oh, I want him to stand on the board so bad…"

I agreed. "This is his first session of the day?" I said, trying to be encouraging. "He's going to stand. For sure."

While the volunteer and Nate waited for another wave, I scanned the waterline towards the Cape, seeing Skye sliding down a sizable wave. After making the drop, she attempted a twirl on the board and fell into the whitewash. I spotted Kami Lambert just a few yards away, said farewell to Michele, and walked over.

"A spin move?" I said. "That's new."

"I was surprised, too!" Kami responded.

"So, I meant to ask you about Skye's speech, before that mandatory water break interrupted us," I reminded Kami.

"Well, at first, she didn't speak," Kami recalled. "To communicate what she wanted, she would use photographs of familiar objects that my mom put together for her on a key ring. It was only after starting Verbal ABA therapy that she got words. Her first 20 words took a long time to get out, and then she slowly added more until she began using simple sentences at four. And remember the typical average is for kids to start mimicking around 10–11 months."

"It just seems like one gigantic, difficult puzzle," I observed.

She nodded. "It is. She did a lot of stimming, at first. She would flap her hands and hum constantly. So when we put her on the gluten and casein-free diet, the humming, the happy feet, and the stimming stopped."

While I knew the intricacies of a gluten-free diet, I had never heard of a casein-free diet. I would later find out that casein is a type of protein found in dairy products.

"We started all the interventions at the same time, just like they tell you *not* to do…but we did it because, in the moment, you want nothing more than to help your kid. The doctor even told us to try stopping the diet to see if it was really the source of the positive change. So we did—which had its own difficulties, since she was used to eating that way. And once we took her off, the humming started all over again."

In front of us, Skye took the last wave of the session and, navigating the crowded arena with ease, she slid to the bottom of the wave before launching into another dance on the surfboard, falling again and coming up smiling.

"What's her exact diagnosis?" I asked.

"She's on the higher functioning end of the spectrum," Kami explained. "Her official diagnosis is mild-to-moderate autism."

"And her biggest struggle?"

She answered without hesitation. "Anxiety. You can see the social awkwardness—typical teenagers don't act like her. She's friendlier. That's not a bad thing at all, but she's naïve and a lot younger than her peers in certain areas. She can also get really repetitive. For example, right now everything is about dogs and pop music."

Skye approached us after helping a volunteer place the surfboard with the others on the sand in preparation for the next heat. She looked upset, confused, and heartbroken, which was noticeably strange given that she'd seemed to be having a blast in the surf session.

"Momma, who is this?" Skye asked, the beginnings of tears in her eyes.

"Skye, this is Cash," Kami replied. "You don't remember Cash from the last events?"

Skye looked at me, then zipped her eyes over to her mother. Then back at me, and then towards Kami again. I had no inkling of what would happen next.

Voice shaky, she asked, "Does this mean you're not going to be with Papa anymore?"

Kami and I locked eyes and somehow kept straight faces.

"Skye, what are you talking about?" Kami ask. "Papa is my man. You know that!"

Skye's head dropped, and she turned to walk towards the family tent.

The moment she was out of earshot, I doubled over laughing, tears streaming down my face.

"That came out of nowhere! What was that about?" I asked.

"I'm stunned," Kami said, laughing hysterically, too.

The ice more than broken, I asked Kami the fundamental question I was seeking to answer: how surfing has been therapeutic for children like Skye.

"What we have found with surfing is that it allows Skye to decompress," she began to explain. "It is a tremendous stress reliever. She does become calmer and happier. She has a lot of anxiety; in fact, that's what gives her some of the most difficulty with autism. Anxiety makes her have behavior issues—anger, lashing out verbally, picking fights with us, meltdowns, paranoia—all of which, of course, makes her feel awful."

But something different happens when Skye surfs.

"When she is lying on her board in the water, watching and feeling the rhythm of the waves, catching them, riding them to the shore and paddling out again, over and over, I don't think she's thinking about things that make her anxious," Kami continued. "When surfing, she lives in the moment, not dwelling on past instances when things went wrong or worrying about what might happen in the future. She is in the now."

She *is* in the now—in her zone, on her game, focused.

Kami then touched on another interesting topic—how, when faced with unpredictable, powerful waves, the participants that surf still confront the challenge head on—literally.

"Even when she catches a wild wave, she is in control of how she deals with it. I think she feels powerful and strong, capable and calm. Nature therapy, water therapy, and sport therapy at its best. Thank goodness for surfing—it truly has been a godsend."

With Kami following Skye's footsteps towards the family tent, I waved goodbye and spent the remainder of the session looking to invade the tents of the frequent fliers I had met thus far.

At the Cocoa Beach event, I was finally able to settle into a rhythm with these surf events. Similar to going to a theme park or a festival, the first event you attend is about experiencing everything. You don't want to miss out on anything being offered—the volunteer meetings, talking with other volunteers, taking the participants surfing, seeing a breakthrough firsthand, checking out the merchandise tent, talking with Don... For the first time, walking the waterline, I didn't feel the usual urge to rush to the next exciting moment. I was still taking everything in, but at a less exhausting pace. I watched Skye, Damian, and Nate surf to a soundtrack of crashing waves and cheers; Miranda and Byron, though hard to pinpoint, were constantly streaking by with participants and surfboards; I met the frequent fliers during the Laura Fuentes-organized lunch as they scooped food onto my plate; and Don cheered and pointed at participants riding waves into shore as he ran through the waterline, sporting a t-shirt with the SFA logo proudly emblazoned on it.

Remembering Don's promise to land a helicopter near the event site, I took a break from the water action and trudged through the hot sand and along the long boardwalk to a grassy field at the nearby beach park, where a helicopter sat waiting. Excited participants were taking turns sitting in it, examining the cockpit; other participants were painting over the "Cocoa Beach" banner on police cars. A firetruck had lifted its crane to the sky, showering water on other participants below.

Even at a glance, it was clear to anyone that this wasn't just a surf event—it was a festival.

SFA had learned how to create an event with so many facets that it is, to some degree, indescribable. The truth is this: there's more excitement and energy to be found at this kind of event than at a theme park.

"A, B, C…"

"A, B, C, D, E…"

"A, B, C, D, E, F, G…"

At some point, I expected Michele or her husband Chris to pry the singing children's book away from Nate's grasp, given the circumstances. But neither made a move to do so.

Sliding into in the driver's seat of the Weppner's SUV, and absolutely melting in the Florida summer night heat, I began hitting every button in reach in an attempt to find the headlights.

"Someone hit the AC before this thing explodes," bellowed Chris from the backseat, where he sat between Nate and Daniel. While I was hysterically laughing at Chris's comment, Nate let the alphabet melody hit Z, before starting up again at A.

It had been "months" since Michele and Chris had a chance to let loose at the bar, or so they said, and the afterparty the night following the surf action at the Cocoa Beach event represented a chance to unwind. Hosted at an open-air restaurant near the water with dolphins playfully splashing in the distance, the afterparty served as their bender.

We had been one of the last groups to leave the restaurant, where a host of families, from the Weppners to the Poes, the Fuentes, Kami and Skye, the Arnolds, Don, and Kim, had spent a pleasant evening laughing, singing, and dancing, all the while conversing about each child's surf experience that day.

Five minutes into the drive, Michele remarked "Cash, I think we're going the wrong way."

"This should spit us out onto the main drag at Atlantic Ave," I responded, utterly lost but maintaining my confidence.

"A, B, C, D, E, F, G..."

"The bed at that hotel was so thick," Michele said over the noise in the car, the atmosphere still humid and hot as the A/C kicked in. "Nate jumped on it for two hours, so it's probably good and flat at this point. Hey, think they have any fanny packs in here for my sea shell collection?"

"H, I, J, K, L, M, N, O, P..."

I slowed down as we passed the iconic Ron Jon Surf Shop, which Michele had pointed out. Lit up like the Las Vegas strip, the well-known two-story shopping center capitalizes on surfing merchandise, from stickers to surfboards, skateboards, and t-shirts. Inside, the smell of cigarette smoke is ever-present, and the whole structure has a transient loneliness to it.

"Q, R, S, T, U, V..."

"Fifty cents for a beer?" said Chris from the backseat, eyeing more signs along the main drag. "Hey baby, let's get on over there."

"W, X, Y, Z...."

We finally pulled into the hotel parking lot. Everyone disembarked, with Nate jumping out last. As soon as he did, Daniel grabbed his hand and led him towards the hotel room. Michele gave me a quick hug, Chris thanked me for my help that day, and Daniel waved a quick goodbye. As I walked towards my hotel room, almost swimming through the thick humidity in the air, I realized that, even though I had met them only recently, they already felt like family.

〰〰〰

"Boy, the sand got hot yesterday," said Don, pulling up a chair beside me. "Did you see me wearing my socks?"

We were sitting under a tent outside a tattoo shop near the Cocoa Beach highway the following day, as Mark Longnecker and crew offered discounts on specific SFA tattoos, with proceeds deposited back into the organization's pockets. Tracy Bastante and Laura Fuentes were already inside.

I had just returned from eating brunch with Byron, Christine Poe, and a few other families and volunteers. When I first woke up—sunburned and sore—I didn't have any plans, so Byron was quick to offer me an invitation.

A consistent flow of passersby kept the conversation between Don and I light and sporadic, as parents and children alike bid goodbye to "the Don" and thanked him for the weekend, promising to attend the next event a few weeks later near St. Petersburg.

"It's amazing how the events take my mind off...well, me," I said to Don during a lull in foot traffic. "In the big scheme of things, there's so many other people going through so many other things."

"Sometimes we take for granted how good we really have it," Don replied, his tone soft and grandfather-like. "Then you get injected into this arena and you're forced to back up and say, 'Wow. Okay, I don't have it so bad.'"

Another family infiltrated the tent, hugging and thanking him. I scanned the group of people outside the tattoo shop, looking for anyone I recognized, overwhelmed by the dedication I saw on hand.

To attend an SFA event hours away from home is dedication enough; but to spend the day after the event, a Sunday, with the same crew, setting up tents outside of a tattoo shop in the sweltering summer heat, keeping up conversations about struggles from the previous day, and even injecting permanent ink into their skin for a cause, floored me.

But, as I was just beginning to understand, such an emotion was the natural result of traveling up and down Florida's coast with a vibrant community, bound together by surfing and autism.

7

WHAT MAKES SURFING THERAPEUTIC?

"Where else can you deface county or city property and not be arrested for it? Surfers for Autism. You can paint a fire engine legally and they're glad to have you."

I n the week leading up to the fifth stop on the 2015 Surf Tour, which was slated to take place on a beach just outside St. Petersburg, FL, the surf report looked dismal. While Florida's Atlantic coast of sees swell after any hint of activity in the Atlantic, it takes specific low-pressure systems or hurricanes to create surf-able swell in the Gulf of Mexico. Neither were on the forecast.

The reality that early summer sees few major hurricanes on average in Florida, and thus the least amount of swell during the year, meant that the stage was set for an SFA event in flat water.

This brought up a question that I'd posed to Don Ryan before, on multiple occasions: Why hold surf events in areas where there are no waves?

Don very politely put a stop to my ignorance: "Children can, from past experience putting on such events, receive similar therapeutic benefits even without the wave itself, or while on a paddle-board."

His response piqued my interest, and I decided to hunt for research on the therapeutic properties of water.

I had experienced the therapeutic properties of water already, at least to some degree. There had been multiple instances when, after jumping into the ocean, a lake, or a pool, I simply felt better; more relaxed, more present. Not to mention, I'd been completely hooked on surfing since the first moment I stood on a surfboard, sliding down a wall of solid water at Waikiki Beach—the Mecca of surfing.

The point is, surf therapy isn't new to our culture. In fact, there are tens of organizations, "from sea to shining sea," that take participants surfing, from those with special needs to military members with PTSD and more. The resounding result is that the participants smile from ear to ear, and experience specific therapeutic benefits. They too become hooked.

In the book *Blue Mind: The Surprising Science That Shows How Being Near, In, On, or Under Water Can Make You Happier, Healthier, More Connected, and Better at What You Do*—published in 2014—author Wallace J. Nichols, a scientist/researcher, devotes 260 pages, with over 40 pages of references and citations, to scientific studies on the question of why water is therapeutic, injecting commentary on topics including why we're drawn to water in the first place, why we respond to its beckoning color so well, and how exactly it can make us feel better. More than anything, the text seems to signify that research on water and the true effects of its healing properties, much like in the autism field, is ever expanding. According to Nichols, there's science behind why your first surf experience can hook you—something many of the participants on the Surf Tour experienced:

> ...*Dopamine release is associated with novelty, risk, desire, and*
> *effort activity; it's also a key part of the system by which the*

brain learns. All of these factors, Zald points out, are present in surfing: "As surfers are first learning, there's an amazing burst of dopamine simply when they stand on the board"...Novelty? Check. Risk? Check. Learning? Check. Aerobic activity? Check. Dopamine? In spades." But that's not all...aerobic exercises (such as surfing) produce endorphins, the opioids that affect the prefrontal and limbic areas of the brain involved in emotional processing, and create the feeling of euphoria, known as runner's high. The beauty of the natural environment where people surf also increases the sense of a peak emotional experience. Add the dopamine, the endorphins, and the natural setting to the adrenaline rush produced by the amygdala's "fight or flight" impulse when a surfer is faced with a large wave (or a wave of any kind when you're first starting out), and you've got a seriously addictive experience.[1]

Before the Pass-A-Grille event, I dug further into Nichols' work to find out how water, surfing, and even just being on a surfboard can be therapeutic for children with autism:

There are all kinds of theories about why this happens. The water is stimulating visually, which fulfills some children's sensory needs; water provides "a safe and supported environment" that surrounds the body with "hydrostatic pressure" that "soothes and calms" (as another expert said, it feels like the "ultimate hug"). Learning new motor skills like swimming, surfing or paddle-boarding can have "a broad ranging impact on the nervous system," according to William Greenough at the Beckman Institute at the University of Illinois: "There's increased blood flow to crucial neurons, and the reshaping of abnormal structures in the front brain. But beyond that, surfing may be a vehicle to an emotional breakthrough, a way of reaching under the mask and perhaps connecting to kids like these." Trying to balance and ride waves also provides them with a clear focus and keeps them in the present moment—neurobiologist Peter Vanderklish believes that the beauty of surfing "turns the focus of these kids inside out. They're pulled out of themselves by having to live in the moment, and all their anxieties push aside."²

This fascinating research begins to paint a picture on an otherwise blank canvas as to why surfing and water do indeed aid in a progression of sorts, as well as how water can help children on the spectrum say their first words.

It offers an explanation for why a select number of families—namely the Fuentes, the Weppners, the Arnolds, Poes, Kami and Skye, as well as Tracy and Damian—forego vacation days and finances and follow the Surf Tour for 13 weeks out of the year.

As I flipped through the pages, I discovered the California born-and-bred author also gives specific mention to one organization that helps children with autism surf:

…It's on the beach, in the waves that some of the biggest transformations take place. In Deerfield Beach, Florida, a fit, white-haired, fiftyish surfer dude named Don Ryan has been running a program called Surfers for Autism since 2007. Professional surfers and other volunteers come together with around two hundred autistic kids and their families for a day of surfing, paddle-boarding, music and games. Children with many of the classic traits of autism—including lack of ability to focus, limited communication skills and ability to verbalize, anxiety around others, lack of social skills and inappropriate response, difficulty forming personal attachments, a sense that they are in their own world, and extreme sensitivity to light, sound, smell, repetitive movements and ritualistic behavior—often approach

the water with fear and trepidation. But time and time again, once they're in the water, or on a surfboard or paddle-board, something good happens. Kids who have rarely smiled or spoken wear wide grins as they ride a wave to shore. They come out themselves and start to relate to people around them. Dave Rossman, who volunteers with the group, comments, "Once they are on the beach, you can't tell a kid with autism from any other child." One mother at a Surfers for Autism event said, "I will never forget the joy I saw on my daughter's face that day the pride she felt that she was enough just the way she was." At these events, her daughter "isn't a girl with Asperger's—she's just a girl who is seven, catching a wave."[3]

"No way, that's awesome!" said Don Ryan, standing in the cool sand of Pass-A-Grille, the beach just outside of St. Petersburg that served as the next stop on Tour. Tents were being constructed on the beach during the sunrise hours, and in front of us was a glassy, calm sea looking completely untouched, like a hidden mountain pass after a night's snow.

"I didn't know we were in there," Don mused. "Be sure to get me a copy!"

I nodded, stepping back to respect Don's busy early morning routine at these events, which consisted of delegating where the collection of tents go, coordinating with others to get the 50-plus surfboards out of the two SFA trailers onto the sand, and meeting and greeting seemingly every participant, newcomer, and family member.

Over an hour and a half later, the cool morning and its ambiance had disappeared, and it was standing room only on the snow-colored sand near the SFA main hub tent. With the volunteer meeting only moments away, the water had begun to show a hint of wind skimming over its surface, and the air felt electric, the heat heavy.

SFA frequents had already made their appearances: the Poes, Fuentes, Arnolds, and Damian and Tracy had set up family tents in the growing alleyway down the beach that, like the skyline due north, stretched farther than the eye could see.

Don came over on the mic, pumping up the crowd. "The mayor is so excited to volunteer, I just signed her up!" he bellowed after a call to arms for volunteers.

It turned out that, when Don went to City Hall in St. Petersburg asking if they were interested in hosting the event, people came out of the woodwork to help make it happen, with no one more enthusiastic than the Mayor, Maria Lowe.

"Thank you, Mayor, we love you!" Don was saying, before drawing everyone's attention to the "elephant on the beach."

"I hope everyone's noticed what the Sheriff's Department sent over in the parking lot behind us?"

Like most of those in the crowd, I already had. On the street, which was blocked off for this event, sat multiple armored trucks that looked to have been imported directly from the U.S. military's warehouses in Iraq and Afghanistan.

"They have the doors open for you; you can step right in and put sand on the floor inside, it's absolutely gorgeous." He gestured further out. "We're painting fire engines on the street, too. Because where else can you deface county or city property and not be arrested for it? Surfers for Autism. You can paint a fire engine legally and they're glad to have you."

I silently hoped at least one of the many reporters and news crew members on the scene—I had seen multiple regional media outlets attend each event—caught this line and would use it in their stories.

After that, Don got down to the basics, explaining the goal of today's event to all the gathered volunteers. "We've found out that our kids can get the same benefit—therapeutically speaking—on flat water as with overhead waves. So the plan is, we're going to get after it, stopping at noon.

"When that happens, enjoy responsibly. This is not a Bud Light commercial," Don joked. "Don't eat rack of ribs, four slices of pizza, and drink a jug of sweet tea and expect to get back into the Gulf of Mexico, no strings attached. We're looking at record heats today, so keep a hat on, use sunscreen and be on lookout for each other."

Less than half an hour later, the first heat entered the water and I found myself standing next to Tracy Bastante as Damian began a simulation of wave surfing in the flat Gulf sea.

I tried to describe for Tracy what it had been like to camp with Byron, the Poes, and others the night before at one of the local campgrounds:

"They had one big cabin last night," I said with a laugh. "Byron and I just had a tent with a section of grass, and between the heat, Byron's snoring, and laying on the hard ground all night, I can't say I got a great night's sleep."

Tracy laughed, even as she kept her eyes on Damian. His volunteer team, who stood in chest-high water about 20 yards away from the sand, suddenly bolted towards shore, pushing the board faster and faster.

Damian's curly locks bounced as he popped up from a prone position. After throwing his hands forward in typical surfing-balance fashion, he switched his footing back and forth while a team of volunteers pushed him into shore at a run, aiming to recreate a wave-like feeling.

This exercise was being replicated by the 49 other teams spread throughout the surf zone, as parents cheered and took photos of participants standing proudly. Those special needs participants who were given a paddle-board instead of a surfboard paddled around the same zone, about 25–30 yards offshore, as master volunteers rode the tail of the monster, ten-foot boards.

As Damian's team began another round of the circuit, a bizarre scene was unfolding offshore, catching the eyes of both Tracy and I. Someone was standing on a wakeboard, but the wakeboard wasn't on the water. Instead, it was 15 feet in the air, somehow tethered to a jet ski that sat below it, the two machines connected by what looked to be a hose. It looked like something out of the Matrix trilogy.

Like other teams, Damian and his volunteers turned to view the device, known as a flyboard, which looked to be part of the "rock star" show.

After thoroughly discussing the dangers of the flyboard ("How do you even get on the thing? How do you not fall?"), Tracy shifted the conversation to what had been a hot topic at the previous event in Cocoa Beach—sharks.

"I was watching this show, and it was saying that Florida is the number one state for shark *bites*, but not fatalities," she said. "So I'm driving here, thinking, 'At least the Gulf will be less infested,' only to hear that this great white shark named Katharine that they've been tracking is in the Gulf right now!"

I laughed, all the while keeping my eyes on the action in the sea.

"You know, some people ask me why I let Damian watch these shark shows. It's so he knows to be aware of the sharks. If one ever bites your foot, I tell him, 'You punch it in the nose and swim like hell.'"

I was happy to have casual conversation with Tracy, because like with the other families, a bond was growing. With that bond came trust, and with trust I felt more comfortable asking deeper questions about their stories.

Music echoed through the speakers on shore as Damian continued his circuit, waiting for the team to begin pushing, then popping up rapidly into his stance, eyes focused on shore and either switching his feet or walking on the board until the team ran out of water. Then he plopped back onto his belly as the group headed out again, all the while navigating around the other participants, each following the same formula. I found myself impressed by his muscle memory.

After the first session wrapped up and those in the green, flat sea emptied back onto the sand, Byron approached Tracy and me while holding hands with a boy that I'd seen at previous events, often wearing headphones to block out the noise. The memory clicked into place: he was a non-verbal participant, about six years old, that Miranda and I helped surf in Deerfield Beach.

"Come on, let's go!" Byron called in my direction.

I followed him, the boy, and another volunteer out into the ocean. Once we'd waded far enough offshore and found a less crowded area, Byron hoisted the boy from his arms onto the board and positioned him. "Okay, bud, here we go. Up, Up, Up!"

The boy held onto Byron and the other volunteer for balance as he slowly began to stand. Meanwhile, I held the board steady in the flat water.

"Easy bud, don't lean," advised Byron. "Balance yourself, balance yourself! Look, your mom is watching!"

I let go of the board and began to backpedal, predicting the team's movement as they began charging towards the beach with the boy beginning to feebly stand, his tiny legs and knees shaking, his mouth stretched wide with joy and his eyes closed.

As I reached the sand ahead of the team, I came in earshot of his mother saying, "Now he stands on the footstools at home to practice surfing…"

But the rest of her words were drowned out by Byron's booming voice saying, "To the beach, fast, fast, fast! Stay with it, bud! You gotta wanna stay up!"

After I realized my hands weren't really needed and that the boy could balance without me physically holding the board steady, I elected to stay on shore and speak with the mother.

"Our first event was 2013, at Ponce Inlet," she said, after I asked about her son's introduction to SFA. "We went to events in 2014, too. If you had asked him, he would have said no to the events, but now you can't get him out of the water when he gets here. We got to surf with Byron in Stuart when the waves were crazy, and he was surfing around all the other participants in the water and having as much fun."

I was quickly learning that several of the families sought Byron out to take their child surfing. Like Miranda, his motivation and willingness to give the participants his full 100% made him a hot commodity.

"He seems to enjoy every second of it," I said to his mother.

"Oh, he loves it. The first time out, he loved it," she said with a smile. "Then we went to Naples, and during our third event the volunteer on the surfboard was bear-hugging him the entire time. He finally relaxed, and by the end of it he was in the water most of the day. That's what I like the most about these events: the volunteers work with where you're at, at that moment in time. He is big for his age—he's six—but his developmental speech is around three or four. But his balance is really good, and so is his core, because he bounces on a ball whenever we're sitting."

"When was he diagnosed?" I asked.

"It was at three and a half," she responded. "We were struggling with the school system and took him to a developmental pediatrician. We were suspicious; he wasn't talking at all, and the way he played with things…"

"I remember Miranda and I taking him out in the morning at Deerfield Beach this year," I said. "He was making so many noises, just really excited to be out in the water."

"He can talk at home," she said, "but out here it's harder. He's always been cautious to try new things, like climbing stairs and basic childhood things."

"So is surfing an outlet for him? Have you seen progress, any therapeutic benefits?" I asked.

"There really has been," she replied. "He's started talking more, fewer outbursts; it really had a calming effect on him. His language is picking up and we're working on sentences now. He can say his name, though he says it so soft that no one can hear him. Last year we had to work on high-fives. He can't quite do the shaka yet, but we're working on it…"

I smiled, amazed that a child could want so badly to learn how to do a shaka, a greeting and goodbye symbol birthed from Hawaii of "hanging loose"—rather than any of the other things he must have seen on TV shows or the Internet. To me, it showed just how much he revered surfing and this community.

"Hey, can you give me a hand with this?" I heard someone ask from behind me.

I turned to find the owner of the voice and their requested responsibility. It was an SFA frequent flier, one I'd met before—he'd helped Byron and me eat most of the s'mores at the previous night's bonfire.

The volunteer was holding a surfboard next to a tall, thin female participant who looked no older than 11 or 12, with visible physical limitations. She was standing with a woman who was presumably her mother, who looked excited.

The girl couldn't stop moving and twitching. After quick introductions and handshakes, the three of us waded into the sea. Immediately upon touching the water, the girl looked tight and nervous. Her eyes were wide with fear of the unknown. Despite her initial reluctance to get on the board and wade in with us, she finally plopped on after some coaxing. Yet even with the other volunteer's convincing, she remained on her belly until we reached the sand on the first push of the circuit. We saw progress on the second try, as she slowly collected herself into a kneeling position…and then dropped back onto her stomach.

On the third try, she made use of an unorthodox tool to aid in her balance—the volunteer's bald head. She rose to a kneel and, after palming the volunteer's scalp with her left hand and placing her right hand in mine, her shaky frame rose and rose...until she was standing, laughing, and snorting.

We immediately ran her and the board into shore, as if she was surfing a wave, where her mother was already cheering, applauding, and snapping photos of the girl, who was beaming.

With every repetition, the girl's balance and confidence grew. We completed circuit after circuit with the girl holding onto the volunteer's bald head for stability. After the buzzer sounded, I locked eyes with the other volunteer. We both grinned and pushed her on one last ride.

The more time I spent near the blonde-haired, Converse-wearing, pink-clad Christine Poe—who had also stayed at the camp grounds with her family the night before—the more I began to hear a certain phrase: "Can you watch my boys for just a second?"

The answer was always a resounding yes. How could anyone say no to spending a few minutes with such energetic boys? Their consistent level of excitement doesn't even hint at their difficult beginnings.

"I had them at 31 weeks—the average is 40, you know," Christine explained. "They were so premature, the doctors told me odds were that their brains wouldn't be fully developed. So we knew they'd be delayed; it's heartbreaking but at the time I was happy they were alive. We were in the NICU, of course; Ethan was in for seven weeks and Evan eight weeks. I had to go back and forth, leaving my oldest, Abbey, at home.

"A full-term baby goes home at about seven pounds. But when I brought them home from the hospital, Ethan was about 4 pounds, 5 ounces; he'd only gained a pound and half in two months."

"What is it like to have a double dose of autism?" I asked.

"You think, 'Why did this happen to me?' You see other people's lives, and they look so much easier. You get a little 'woe is me.' Sometimes, it just plain sucks. But I'm blessed to have them. And at some point, you have to put your big-girl panties back on."

For the Poes, surfing became an integral part of their lifestyle, along with other forms of therapy. "My boys, they think it's a part of life," Christine told me. "They've always loved the beach. That's Ethan's calm place; he could go all day boogie boarding. And Evan, when he's on the beach, he doesn't have disagreements with the other kids. They both love being told they're 'surfer boys,' and living the surfer image. Ethan stood up on a surfboard for the first time in Cocoa Beach four years ago, and it took Evan two years to stand up. Everybody was cheering for him because he had finally done it! I even cried."

When I spotted the brothers at that day's event, they were already in the placid sea outside of the surf zone, sporting blue SFA rash guards, snorkels and boogie boards. Although Ethan barely noticed when I jumped in beside the two, Evan immediately paddled my way on the boogie board, holding onto it since he was unable to touch the sandy bottom below.

"PUSH ME! PUSH ME! PUSH ME!" he yelled.

There was no arguing with that. I grabbed the board and started sprinting through the chest-high water into the shallows. Evan, his mask covering most of his face, got a mouthful of water in the process because he couldn't stop laughing. After multiple twirls and pushes, he finally found footing in the water.

"You're, you're, you're my best friend," he blurted out.

"I am? Why me?" I asked.

"You've been to my house and, and we played video games together and, and, and we have your towel!" he exclaimed.

Evan was right—months prior, I was driving through the family's city on Florida's west coast and asked if I could stop by. Bob and Christine were in overwhelming agreement, and I spent the majority of the afternoon with Evan teaching me how to play his favorite video game, while Ethan elected to play games on a different device nearby. I didn't ask any questions about autism; instead, I simply enjoyed feeling like a part of the family.

"Oh, my towel with the map of Las Vegas on it? I think you guys took it after an event by accident. Do you and your mom and dad use it?" I jokingly asked.

"Yeah! Well, we, we, we were just borrowing it," he answered.

"You've borrowed it for over a year," I said, trying to hide my grin.

"Well, that's because, that's because some people borrow stuff for a year," he shot back.

"So you like to borrow things for over a year?" I asked him, keeping the back-and-forth going.

"Yeah!" he said. "I don't like, I don't like, I don't like, *want* people borrowing things. Because they don't give it back. The stuff."

"Would you let me borrow something?" I asked him, playfully.

"No," he curtly replied.

The conversation became like a volleyball game. "But I let you borrow my towel. And we played video games!"

"Okay."

"So what can I borrow?"

"One of my movies."

"Which one?"

"*Toy Story 3*! I have it. Throw me, throw me!"

With that, I grabbed Evan and launched him into the air, his frame tucking into a ball before exploding into the calm, surrounding water. From the moment I met him, I knew that regardless of any label, he had that rare, intangible quality: kindness.

"Throw me, too!" demanded Ethan, and I obliged by tossing him into the air, snorkel and all.

"Throw me again, again!" said Evan, reappearing.

"I don't want to hurt you," I responded, now kneeling in the water.

"Try!" Evan screamed gleefully.

"Me too, me too!" I heard Ethan say.

After another heave for the two, I decided to trudge into deeper water. I didn't realize that such an act would be taken as a challenge.

"Don't let him get away!" Ethan gurgled, as he and his brother gave chase. Moments later, the two were both laughing and swimming in my direction as if they were two alligators stalking prey. I began to swim away, albeit slowly, and when one of the boys grabbed onto my shoulder, I turned and threw Evan backwards, and then Ethan, and Evan again.

Time after time, they barreled towards me in unison, with one of the boys keeping my attention while the other latched onto my back.

After several minutes, the endgame approached: their father, Bob Poe. The moment he waded into the sea, the boys' hot radar locked on.

"What is this? What are you doing to Cash?" he asked Ethan, who'd approached him first.

"Throw me!" was his only reply, which Bob did, throwing first Evan, then Ethan, and then Evan again. I stepped back to watch as the sea became an arena dotted with mini-explosions of white water centering around Bob.

The scene, lit by the overhead sun and set against the green water and the piped-in audio from the SFA sessions running just a few yards up the beach, combined with the laughter from the two Poe boys, suddenly became a powerful visual in my mind. It was a moment devoid of all labels, all stresses, paperwork, co-pays, frustrations, and past or future difficulties. It was a scene devoid of autism itself.

It was simply a father, enjoying a fleeting moment in time with his two children. After snapping a mental photograph of the scene, I waded onto shore, dripping saltwater. With a newfound sense of hope, I set my steps in the direction of the cheers and applause.

Given the record heat index Don alluded to at the beginning of the day, combined with moisture in the air, it was only a matter of time until a destructive yet beautiful Florida thunderstorm blew in.

One side of the sky began to darken, and less than an hour later the menacing storm system was hovering over the event site. During the lunch break, thunder shook the sand, and the sky violently let loose. The closest shelter I could find was in the Arnolds' Florida Gators tent.

Its top was lowered to weather the storm, and as I approached, only Keith Arnold's feet were visible.

After discussing the weather with Keith, the conversation shifted onto the common bond I'd discovered I had with the Arnolds: we both shared an affinity for travel, for leaving the known and experiencing the unknown. As if he was a well-known friend, we traded travel stories and trips we wanted to embark on.

After half an hour of conversation, the ominous clouds parted and sunshine took its place. Don gave the green light for participation to resume, and as I emerged from under the tent, feeling like a family in the Midwest slowly climbing out of their storm cellar, the scene looked shockingly the same as it had before the storm: the rows of tents remained, along with hundreds of thousands of fresh footprints. In fact, the volunteer chute was already filled with double-digit numbers of special needs participants, ready to surf. I doubted that everyone would leave, though I did imagine some of the crowd calling it quits. But it was obvious to all that today was a beach day unlike any other during the year.

The surf sessions continued, with more and more participants being pushed on simulated waves—some standing, others making progress by simply entering the ocean. There were cheers from the beach crowd and there were meltdowns (which Byron often tried to address); all in all, business as usual for an SFA event, despite the lack of surf.

By the time the last session of the day had ended, the sky had completely cleared from cloud cover and the sauna-like humidity had returned, as the group ebbed back towards the SFA-sponsored hotels just across the street.

After quick naps and showers—and for me a quick return to the campsite to pack up—a large crew of volunteers, participants, and SFA frequent fliers met up to eat together at the beachside restaurants. For dinner, everyone gathered to watch the last light of day sinking into the watery horizon. To say the sunset was magnificent would be an understatement: rays of orange and yellow exploded across the sky.

An hour later, as we sat in the darkness, families began saying goodbye to friends. I did the same, hugging the other volunteers whom I felt so close to, yet whom I had only met that morning. The entire moment felt like the end of a family reunion.

8

THE SURF FAMILY

"You feel like a superhero when you work with the kids. For 20 minutes, I have a real shot at making a difference in the families' lives."

"That's who he thinks he is. Damian will tell everyone who asks, he's a surfer," said Tracy Bastante, watching on the sands of Ponce Inlet as the first heat paddled into the waist-high offshore waves for the sixth stop on Tour.

Ponce Inlet Jetty is a sliver of salt and sand within Daytona Beach, and although the city is known for its bars, tourism income, and expensive high rises, what's more familiar to most is the storied past time of car racing on the beach's compact, concrete-like, snow-colored sand, as the prestigious Daytona 500 Speedway sits about an hour north.

As the dark night gave way to a soft morning light on the Saturday of the event, the beach transformed from a quiet parking lot with only a handful of cars in sight to a bustling thoroughfare with tire tracks lining the sand. And just 150 yards away from the makeshift road—which even featured speed limit signs—was the sea.

Its beautiful offshore lines were visible from here, forming brown-green, waist-high surf that seemed to fall on top of itself rather quickly with a thunderous, closeout clap. These conditions held throughout the setup, volunteer meeting, and first heat of the day, when Damian paddled out with the assistance of two volunteers.

"Anything, whether it's projects in school or what have you, it's always about surfing," Tracy continued, our conversation centered around how, thanks to SFA, Damian (like so many other participants) could find his identity in surfing. "For a project, he had to create a god or goddess of something, and he said, 'I'm doing a goddess.' Turns out it was one of the girls that volunteers with him. I said, 'Okay, so she's a goddess of what?' He told me, 'Surfing. She helps kids with autism. She teaches me how to stand on the board and ride the waves to the beach and she's my girlfriend.' Then he tells me, 'I need my hair long, I'm with Surfers for Autism.'"

I wanted to know more about Damian's competitive streak outside of SFA events, and Tracy was happy to explain. Every event brings with it updates to a hundred ongoing narratives, as proud mothers can't help but gush about their children and what they've accomplished thanks to being introduced to surfing.

"We have a Special Olympics event next Saturday in Stuart," Tracy told me, as Damian paddled into his own wave and popped up with ease. "He has to get first or second to get to State this year. At another event this past Sunday, he came in fifth; but he wasn't at all into it. I think they judged something wrong, because he jumped and turned on his board. People on the beach were impressed—saying, 'Oh, wow, he does tricks,' but the judges didn't give him any points for it. I've been trying to teach him to be a good sport, but he just says, 'I'm a loser; I came in last place.'"

After a push from a volunteer, Damian popped up and, by leaning more forward on the board, he followed the slope down into a thick wave. Holding his stance as it clamped shut behind him, with an explosion of whitewater acting as a backdrop, he rode the energy towards dry sand.

"Wow, that last drop was awesome!" I heard an onlooker say. I turned around to see a man approaching us, his eyes fixed on Damian.

"Does he do any competition?" the middle-age man asked. His high level of enthusiasm made it clear that this was one of his first SFA events.

Tracy nodded, explaining to the man that Damian did Special Olympics, and giving him a brief version of the conversation we'd just had.

"He's trying to learn how to paddle into the bigger waves," she remarked. "He does have upper body strength and he can paddle in whitewater…I've told him he needs to do more pushups."

But scanning the crowd, it looked like finding room to set up and do push-ups would be an impossible task on the Ponce Inlet beach. Every inch of sand was occupied by a throng of onlookers, as well as waiting participants and their families. The air, humid and heavy, was filled with a chaos of contrasts: screams from children having breakdowns, alongside the highly contagious cheers of the crowd.

Leaving Tracy and Damian behind, I spotted Kami Lambert a few yards away, watching her daughter Skye in the lineup.

As with most of our conversations, Kami had me laughing almost immediately.

"When Skye surfs, she either flirts with the volunteer or she shows off," she said. "I'm trying to figure out which she's going to do today."

I looked out at the water just in time to see Skye drop in on a wave that required a split-second pop up. She landed smoothly, completely in control with her hands thrust skyward. Once the whitewash detonated, rising far above her shoulders, she and the board both surged toward the beach.

"She just did a 360!" Kami exclaimed.

"And almost took out a photographer!" I added, joining other viewers applauding.

Suddenly, an out-of-place mechanical noise filled the air, as a squadron of vintage planes flying in a V-formation appeared over the sea, following the direction of the swell.

Don's voice boomed over the microphone: "Every year, we give these kids an air show—" but the sound of the propellers drowned out anything else he might have said.

Volunteers stopped pushing participants into waves as all eyes turned skyward. As fast as they came, the roaring vintage planes disappeared into the dark clouds forming inland and the surfing resumed.

Like most of the crowd, I didn't know where they came from or how Don had organized the flyover. Regardless, I was struck yet again by the profound love being shown for these kids. Like a father proudly gifting his son with new experiences, those holding the reigns at SFA wanted to give the participants and their families a day they would never forget. When put into practice, this theme is easy to do…at least, every so often. But as I've seen firsthand, this theme of "unforgettable moments" is the case at every single event. And it's not just the airshows or the opportunity to paint firetrucks; it's the volunteers, the free food, the camaraderie, the attention to safety and detail. While it can be a busy environment, it's also very peaceful: everything is taken care of for the families so that all attention can be focused on their child's surfing.

After Skye completed several more successful 360 rides in the heavy but clean conditions, I turned to find Michele Weppner sitting in the sand, her feet bathing in a tide pool. The air around her was loud with Nate's "oooooooohs" and "aaaaaaahs," while Daniel held onto Nate's hand.

From our elevated position on the sand, we could keep our eyes on the scene in front of us: the beach, crowded with a throng of people, all standing at the waterline; the tide sweeping at ankles and knees; hundreds more buzzing around the tents to our right.

I asked what the family's plans were for the remainder of the Surf Tour.

"This is our last event as a family, since Daniel starts football soon," Michele said in a relaxed tone.

I didn't respond immediately, momentarily lost in the realization that Michele and I, two complete strangers, were now comfortable enough to sit and talk as friends; and that the source of our bond was the confluence of surfing and autism. We silently watched the action for a few minutes.

"Do you see Abigail down there surfing?" she asked. "I've been watching her this whole time."

I shifted my eyes back toward the waterline and, after scanning the crowd, I spotted a distant figure flapping her arms wildly, wiggling off a surfboard and spilling into the sea. Three volunteers were beside her, repeatedly plucking her out of the water and placing her back on the board. A set of parents and a dog stood directly in front of the group, observing.

"I saw the most precious photo of Abigail on Facebook recently," I said. "It was one of those Timehop photos that the family was tagged in. It showed Abigail sliding down a wave after both Don and Asa pushed her, way back in 2011."

Again, I became lost in my own thoughts, remembering the beach that day. I recalled a cameraman documenting the day for the Maass family; in the video, adorable Abigail ran and jumped in the sand, surfed, and was hoisted into the air by dripping volunteers. She even gave Don Ryan a high five.

"I didn't see Isaiah with you this morning. Where is he?" I asked SFA frequent flier Asa Maass after a handshake. Asa was standing at the waterline with Abigail's beautiful flat-coated retriever Maverick, a well-known service dog at events.

The Maass' were the last family I would spend significant time with on this tour, listening to their story and their experiences with Surfers for Autism. They had attended events for years, eventually becoming a part of the community. In fact, many SFA photos and banners show little Abigail sliding on the waves.

"My mom and stepdad live in North Carolina, so Priscilla and I sent him to visit," Asa replied. "They got to go to the races last night, actually; the Friday night races. Sometimes the monster trucks are really big pick-ups or whatever someone feels like destroying."

This was part of my method—making small talk before getting into any serious questions. That way, not only could we warm up to the topic; I could also learn more about the family—and, in this case, Asa.

As Asa continued, I was reminded of why I loved speaking with him so much. He was a man's man, interested in taking machines apart to see how they run. Every conversation we'd had, other than discussions about Abigail, included football, cars, and all things Southern. I expected this chat would be no different.

"Back in Virginia, we had a track where all you had to do was pay $20 and you could race head to head with someone," he continued. "Back in the 90s, my dad took out my stepmom's '97 Grand Prix. Beat everybody. It was awesome."

In front of us, the volunteers helped Abigail rise to a stand close to shore.

"So you ready for football season?" I asked, aware of where his allegiance lay.

He scowled. "I canceled my Sunday ticket. Every time I pay to see the Redskins, they do terrible. It's a waste of money to watch that much to watch them lose."

Maverick's sudden barking brought us both back to the task at hand, as Abigail rose to a stand before falling back onto the board. The team volunteers kept close so she wouldn't dip off into the sea.

"I may have asked you guys this before, but what was your first event?" I asked, moving the conversation forward.

He answered easily, almost automatically, as if he'd been asked a million times. "Flagler Beach, 2009. Priscilla found SFA on the Internet. We were looking frantically for something to include Abigail in—we'd tried horseback riding, tried cheering, and eventually found this."

The horn immediately sounded and Abigail and her team filed out of the water, with a tall, handsome volunteer bringing her up the beach. She kept her arm locked on the young man. Priscilla had appeared and greeted me in the interim.

"You did great, high-five!" the volunteer said. Abigail put her hand out, her eyes darting back and forth seemingly faster than the speed of light. Seeing her start to shiver, and with lunch coming soon, the family walked towards the city of tents and disappeared.

Post-lunch, the sky grew darker and began to show signs of storms. A high-pitched siren sounded from the lifeguard tower, halting the event.

Thunder began to faintly rumble, and one look at the weather radar on Christine Poe's phone showed a massive blob of yellow shot through with slivers of red. Even though Christine's twin boys weren't at the event, she still wanted to come to be a part of the experience. Strict instructions came from the lifeguard tower: leave the beach or take shelter in a nearby vehicle.

Immediately, Don came over the intercom saying that he and SFA would take shelter momentarily, but that they would plan on waiting out the storm to finish the event.

The city on the beach underwent a rapid deconstruction, as families began moving in the direction of the cars on the sand. Less than 15 minutes later, darkness took over the sky and the heavens opened up; a torrential downpour ensued.

Byron and I took refuge in his nearby vehicle. Sand and water was thrown on the car's floorboard, but Byron didn't seem to care.

While we waited out the storm, sharing stories about the day's surf sessions and breakthroughs, I realized that despite having asked so many other people why they joined the SFA family, I didn't know Byron's reason. So I asked.

It turned out that in 2012, a friend told him about an upcoming event in Tybee Island. Because the friend was so excited about the event, Byron decided to check it out. He loved it so much that he didn't think twice about attending the following event in Jacksonville Beach—he was hooked. So hooked, in fact, that he followed the SFA family to Puerto Rico, the site of another event.

"You feel like a superhero when you work with the kids," Byron said. "For 20 minutes, I have a real shot of making a difference in the families' lives."

But why attend nearly every event instead of a select few?

"I decided to do almost all the events because I love it," he explained. "I love the fact that at every event, you have a real chance of doing something life-changing. I give the kids my time and in return, I get to know that I made a difference. I couldn't think of a better use of my time and extra funds than surfing and hanging out with everyone."

As we continued to wait out the storm, raindrops streaming down the windshield, I was struck by the realization that the combination of surfing and autism is, fundamentally, a match made in heaven.

Whether or not Don and Kim Ryan and the other SFA founders knew it before the first SFA event, gifting surfing to the local autism community was pure genius.

For both groups of people, hope is not a recommendation—it's a requirement. And by that I mean this: hope is an ever-present undercurrent within the surf community in Florida. Certainly the Sunshine State sees plenty of swell; but, as I've stated before, the only consistent thing about the surf in Florida is that it's inconsistent. Quality waves may be forecasted, but they are never guaranteed. Because of this, the foundation of surfing, especially in Florida, sits on a bedrock of unpredictability. That's why surfers exercise hope as a natural aspect of their sport. If there's a hint of swell in the reports, surfers will be at the beach at first light, hoping for one more wave, hoping for one more session. If the surf report is flat, they'll bide their time, hoping for swell in the following weeks, in the following months.

The same attitude can be seen in every SFA member. Whether it is a head-high swell or a flat day, the people of SFA are going to hope, to try. Even if a child is terrified of the ocean, Byron and Keith Arnold and all the other volunteers are going to give him or her a chance to feel the coolness of the sea. Even if the participant doesn't stand on his or her first go, or has yet to stand on a surfboard, the volunteers—most of them Florida surfers, born and raised on hope—are going to try over and over again. Even if they get a few bites in the process.

The wrath of the storm abated after about an hour, and Byron and I climbed out of the car-turned-storm cellar.

The sand, which before had been filled with millions of footprints, was now wet, cold, compact, and new. The sea looked dark and uneasy, almost sickly.

Don emerged, coming over the megaphone to call it a day, and to thank everyone for all the good work. But it didn't seem to put a damper on the mood at all, as a select group of SFA members, including Asa, Alfie, Laura, Byron, Miranda, and a handful of others, put aside the enticing thought of a hot shower at their hotels and helped tear down the signs and remaining tents, and file the dozens of surfboards into their trailers. And all the while, they did so with smiles, laughs, and high energy.

As the remaining vehicles soon departed, all heading in the direction of the afterparty at a beachside restaurant, it became all the more obvious just how tight-knit this group of eclectic families had become, all because of their common bond: being brought together by SFA.

9

THE LAST DAY OF SUMMER

"It's the one thing we all have in common: we all have holes in our wall."

The sky looked dark, but the mood felt far darker. The SFA community was mourning a loss.

As the 5 a.m. set-up began for the next stop on the Tour—Flagler Beach—an unprecedented quietness filled the early morning air, until the only noise heard was the crashing swell somewhere in the distance.

Even though the swell forecast promised some of the best waves the Surf Tour had seen since Cocoa Beach, the only topic of discussion in the days leading up to the event was the passing of Don Ryan's father. Word spread that a memorial paddle out would take precedence on the morning of the event day.

With over half the surfboards heaved down from the trailers, somber SFA members began to quietly but swiftly flow out to the sea. I began to follow suit, picking up an 8-foot green board and venturing towards the waterline. Cold water washed over my feet as I accepted the flowers offered by a silent girl, who proceeded to distribute them to everyone with a surfboard.

After waiting for a lull in the swell, I paddled out, aiming my strokes in the direction of the circle already forming near the pier. Beyond where the waves were breaking, the water looked still, without a blemish on its glassy surface.

I paddled up next to Miranda Fuentes. Her snow-white smile was hidden, and her face was firm and serious. I moved to an upright sitting position, linking hands with her and joining the circle.

Don appeared, floating on a surfboard in the middle of the circle. We were now some 30 yards offshore, with the circle itself stretching 10 or 15 yards wide.

In between controlled sniffles, Don spoke about what his father— his role model, his teacher, his inspiration—meant to him, and how much it meant to have the SFA community present during such a difficult moment.

Then he raised his head, looking around the circle with a burning intensity as he shifted the spotlight onto everyone else. He discussed that inevitable, dreaded point that each of us must one day face, and told those in the circle how best he knew to prepare for it: show love at every opportunity with those you do have in your life.

He paused, before powerfully paddling out of the circle and towards the beach. We tossed our flowers into the middle of the circle and splashed water skyward, our emotions completely uninhibited, fully experiencing the sadness, the loss, and the outpouring of love and respect for Don.

Then it was time for us to disperse as well. We quietly waited for incoming swell, and as I paddled and rode on a wave littered with flower petals towards the beach, I found my mind drifting. Seeing Don take his most painful, most vulnerable moment, and turn it into a teaching lesson for those around him, to me revealed the true and raw strength of his character; a character that has had an impact on so many families and children in Florida and beyond.

I had never before felt this much love at the hand of complete strangers, each united by one common and compassionate thread.

"It's the one thing we all have in common: we all have holes in our wall," said Bob Poe, his eyes focused on his twin boys Ethan and Evan where they bobbed in the sea, halfway through one of the first morning sessions.

Two hours after the memorial paddle out, the waves remained gentle, knee to waist-high watery slopes that might frighten a beginner, but for SFA frequent fliers like Ethan, Evan, Skye and Damian, it was another opportunity to push through any boundaries that stood in their way and grow in their craft.

I enjoyed every conversation I had with Bob Poe. He was genuinely funny, with a penchant for making references to the classic movie *Airplane*, and he was extremely open and inviting. He's the kind of person you could talk to about any situation, and he would offer sound wisdom while injecting just the right amount of humor to make you feel better.

"I didn't see any holes when I came over," I replied. "But I did spend most of my time playing video games with Evan, so…"

"There are two in the dining room and one under the bar," Bob said, thinking. "When we paint, we'll fix the holes—

"Evan! Pull your pants up!" Bob called.

I looked out, and sure enough, whether due to the whitewash or a lack of tension in his shorts, there was Evan exploding towards shore on a wave with his board shorts nearly touching the board. A streak of white stood out in stark contrast with his blue shorts and rash guard.

I couldn't help but laugh. "Now that they're getting older, what's the biggest challenge?" I asked him over the roar of the crowd.

"The behavior is still a big challenge for us," he replied, interrupting himself occasionally to cheer for his sons. "It's a day-to-day thing, like correcting how he eats. Now we're getting into pre-teens… hormones may be a good thing overall, but some of them may not be too fun—like the sexuality hormones. Developmentally, the high school decision is a long way away. I don't know what we'll do about that; I'd say we're hoping to see a bit more calm from Evan, overall. For him, it's about teaching him to recognize the fact that he is not like other kids. He knows he has autism, but now he's starting to ask, 'Why do I have it?'"

"He's asked you that? What did you say?"

"Just that we don't know, but everybody is different," he said. "Everyone has something; yours just happens to be autism. You think differently than the way other people think sometimes, but that's okay. He gets along with the younger kids; our neighbors have an older boy, and he gets it. Thankfully they have a normal sibling relationship. For the most part, they're best friends—"

He stopped, standing up to cheer. "UP, UP, UP, ETHAN! You did awesome, man!"

Ethan flashed us a smile and a quick "Yeah!" before running back towards the volunteers in the sea.

The sand was beginning to feel hot, but the water washing over our ankles provided respite. Bob continued: "High school's a big decision, though. That's what wakes me up at night going, 'Oh my.'

"Plus, I have two more years with Abbey before she goes to school. Then I'll get my new wall of challenges." He sighed. "With school, the boys get structure, and they *do* get excited; that's what can make summer hard. Evan is worried about school and Ethan worries about what Evan is doing. And they're splitting them up in two different classes this year…"

"How is surfing therapeutic for the twins?" I asked.

"There's definitely the social aspect, no doubt," he replied. "When we get to an event, Ethan breaks right out of that shell. Everyone is his best friend. He communicates a lot more than when he first started surfing. Now he has an identity. He's doing something, recognizing it's awesome.

"The social aspect is also important for us as parents, too," he went on, "because we're able to come across people at all different ends of the autism spectrum. Plus, surfing really forces the boys to process things 'in the now.'"

Reminded that I had already asked Christine her thoughts about a double dose of autism, I posed the question to Bob.

"We get a different challenge from both of them each day," Bob said. "It's about putting ourselves in their world and, through trial and error, seeing what helps and what doesn't help."

Bob saw his sons heading back up from finishing their heat. "AWE-SOME boys, great rides! Let's all get a picture. Say thank you to the volunteers!"

Just watching Bob split his focus between cheering on his sons and giving me running commentary of their difficulties had got my adrenaline firing. I was incredibly impressed at how he could look so calm and casual through it all.

As Bob, Ethan, and Evan turned to head off in the direction of the city of tents, I sidestepped through the crowd until I found Kami Lambert standing amidst the throng. Music blasted over the speakers, filling an already excited atmosphere with even more energy and noise.

"Did you see the dolphins this morning after the paddle out?" Kami asked after I said hello. "It was a perfect, gorgeous morning. Beautiful."

"It's something to remember…especially that sunrise," I replied.

In front of us, Skye was pushed onto a wave, made the drop, and using her back foot as if it were a rudder, she expertly wiggled the board in between other participants and volunteers.

As she paddled back out, my eyes caught Lucas Fuentes in the same heat, sliding on a wave in the opposite direction. His tall frame helped him maintain his balance all the way to the sand, even after making a harrowing drop. After watching him navigate the traffic with ease, I smiled, and noticed a dull, almost-familiar ache in my jaw. It took me a moment to realize the cause: I still wasn't used to feeling pain from smiling too much.

"Where, where, where is Ethan?" Evan asked.

"He's fine, Evan, he's in the water and within the play boundaries," his father replied, staying shielded from the blazing summer sun under the family's tent.

I had taken refuge there, as the surf sessions continued outside in the brutal heat. Having already asked about his brother, I started to ask Bob about the challenges he faced with Ethan, when news came in through the grapevine that Christine wasn't feeling well, likely due to the unforgiving heat. Bob cut himself off mid-sentence to go find her, so once again I took on the role of watching the boys.

"Hey, Evan! Let's go play with your brother!" I suggested.

He looked up from digging a hole in the sand, squinted and smiled.

As we headed off to locate Ethan, Evan excitedly started pointing out people he'd met during the event, and it was entertaining to momentarily see the event through his eyes. "Hey, I was playing volleyball with them, I was playing volleyball with them!" he shouted, pointing to a group of three attractive bikini-clad females. I immediately burst out laughing.

Upon seeing an older gentleman by the waterline, Evan's voice suddenly called out: "HELLO BEACH SANTA! HEY BEACH SANTA, WHY DO YOU HAVE THAT SHIRT ON WHY DO YOU HAVE

THAT SHIRT ON I KNOW WHY YOU HAVE THAT SHIRT ON I CALLED YOU IT YOU'RE THE BEACH SANTA!"

"Yes, thank you for my name," replied the previously-christened Beach Santa, an older SFA frequent flier who admittedly does pose as Santa during the holidays. For that reason, he keeps his white beard full year-round and wears red shorts and a white shirt reading "BEACH SANTA."

"You know, he's the first one who called me that, three or four years ago," the Beach Santa confided in me, smiling.

I smiled. "Evan's so funny. I wouldn't be surprised if every person on this beach is friends with him."

No longer interested in Beach Santa or what he received for Christmas last year, Evan had already taken off in the direction of the sea looking for his brother. I followed him down to the waterline outside of the surf zone, and both boys began a repeat of the Pass-A-Grille event, paddling towards me as I continued to toss them back into the sea, one after the other.

Something I didn't expect to see at the event had to do with a lack of localism.

The term in the surfing dictionary carries a negative connotation, and rightly so. Localism is defined as someone having a preference for or allegiance towards a region, or in this case a surf break. It leads to surfers verbally or physically assaulting one another for surfing at a break. In contrast to other action sports, like skateboarding and snowboarding, waves only come every so often (when the right weather conditions line up during a particular season), and as a result the playing field is small and usually crowded.

Because localism is usually driven by more emotion than logic, it can be caused by many things, ranging from dropping in on someone (cutting someone off on a wave) or paddling out into a surf break with friends, immediately crowding the lineup. It can even be based on age: if young surfers (called groms) take "too many" waves, an older surfer may yell at the young guns to show some respect for the older guys. Or, if a surfer paddles out and immediately catches a wave, instead of allowing those who have been waiting in the lineup to catch it, localism—in this case, in the form of a heated conversation—may ensue.

A good amount of the volunteers at the day's event were local surfers, young and old. But interestingly, during the surf sessions, I didn't see any confrontations occur. Participants were pushed on the same waves, but instead of yelling, cheers ensued. If there were any close calls—surfers nearly running into another— apologies were given. If one surfer and volunteer team were the first ones to reach a particular patch of sea, they didn't argue when others infiltrated the same area later on.

The lineup was without even a hint of localism—all because the focus was on helping others achieve the ride of their lives.

I found that one of the things that makes SFA so thrilling is that, simply by walking along the beach, you can find yourself drawn into inspiring conversations.

"She goes to the Jacksonville School for Autism," said Priscilla Maass, who glows every time she's asked about her daughter Abigail.

Because the family wouldn't be at the next event, I planned on spending the following event with them in Jacksonville Beach. Before that though, I wanted to ask a few more questions.

"At school this year, half of the day is clinics, and the other half day is in the classroom. The classroom, of course, is all autism; the clinical side is one-on-one ABA therapy. It's intensive; plus, Abigail does therapy after school as well."

Then, after a few more minutes of conversation, Priscilla ventured off in the direction of the merchandise tent. Such is the nature of discussion at SFA events: quick, sometimes random, liable to stop at a moment's notice with the appearance of a child ticcing and stemming.

Scanning the action-packed waterline for familiar faces, I noticed Laura Fuentes. I refocused on what Laura was looking at: Lucas, lying on a surfboard in the sea front of us, with Alfie holding the tail.

"What's been new with Lucas over the summer?" I asked after exchanging a greeting. I hadn't spoken with Laura in depth recently, so I felt obligated to ask.

"He's been swimming now," said Laura, excitement clear in her voice. "His focus is on competitions. He's a natural, with that perfectly tall and lanky body."

I nodded and smiled in agreement.

"But he wants to go back to school," she continued. "He became a true teenager this summer and adopted the skill of sleeping in. Which is strange; with autism you don't usually get to sleep in! But we've also been working on more of his social teenager skills: doing things like going to the movies with a friend.

"He started texting with a friend, and we were really excited about that. Baby steps, you know? He's been getting job experience, too. His school takes him out to sites, and two days a week he's been shelving at a grocery store. The school's goal is to help create skills by letting them work different places. Though it's a major issue once someone ages out..."

"Aging out" refers to the notion that, with time, every child (with or without autism) will eventually grow too old to attend school. What comes after that, finding that next step, is a source of anxiety for Laura and many other parents who have children with autism. Thus, the goal is to prepare those with autism to begin a career or some form of activity, not only to keep them busy, but to help them earn a living wage and have tasks to accomplish while accompanied by others. You may have heard of stores, restaurants, or companies in your community that hire adults with autism or other special needs—these companies are helping to fill the void, serving as the next step for many of those with autism.

After a few more waves, the horn sounded and the last heat of the day was over. Alfie and Laura, with Lucas in tow, trotted off to begin tearing down the city of tents. Conversations within the sand city centered around arranging rides back to the hotel and to the inevitable afterparty.

I gathered my belongings and joined the families slowly departing from the beach, keeping my footsteps near the cool water.

That's when a flash of color caught my eye. There, near my foot, laying on top of the sand, was a red flower petal—a leftover from the morning's paddle out.

A moment later, the tide swept over it, pulling it back out to sea.

"We took a kid out today. First and second session? It was like night and day," Byron said.

Byron, a few other volunteers and I left the afterparty early (in search of ice cream, as it happened). After finding a beachside creamery, we sat down to enjoy our frozen treats, while I asked whether he'd had any challenging participants during the day's event.

"We had to pick the kid up out of the sand, and during the first session we really had to push him on a couple of rides. But the second time? He got into a rhythm, he was so calm; he was almost falling asleep, and we had to get his attention on a couple rides."

It became obvious, having spent weekend after weekend with SFA, that the parents who call themselves frequent fliers (the Poes, the Maass', the

Weppners, the Fuentes, Arnolds, Kami, and Tracy) have supernatural energy levels.

There's simply no other way to describe the mothers and fathers who can spend all day at the beach in the hot sun and deep sand, cheering for their children and conversing with best friends, only to spend the night drinking and dancing their cares away at a beachside restaurant—and still wake up the following morning for a 7 a.m. breakfast.

But true to form, by 7:01 a.m. the next morning the noise from the lobby restaurant was reaching the upper levels of the sponsored hotel. I could even hear it in the elevator as I rode down from my room.

Once I stepped out of the elevator and into the breakfast area, it looked like the group was already on the verge of spilling out into the street. It looked like standing room only as I slid through a sea of blue SFA t-shirts, looking for an open seat. That's when I noticed the Arnolds sitting in the right corner of the room, waving me over.

I excused myself through the crowd, passing by where Don and Kim stood eating and talking to a new SFA parent.

"Look, did you see this?" said Linda as I sat down next to Keith, across from her and Christopher.

She handed over her phone. On it was a picture of Christopher, beaming while standing with a group of firefighters in what looked to be the lobby of the hotel.

"Cool!" I exclaimed. "Wait. Was this…?"

"This morning!" she nodded. "Someone had burned toast earlier and the fire department came. When Christopher saw the firefighters, he wanted a picture."

"He's trying to get their votes!" I quipped with a laugh and a smile, recalling her referring to Chris as her little politician.

"Did you get any sleep last night?" Keith asked, as I started eying the breakfast buffet.

"A bit," I replied. "I was in Christine Poe's room with Byron, Michele, and others way past midnight just talking. You couldn't walk anywhere inside because people were even sitting on the floor; it was so much fun."

Christopher suddenly stood up. Linda immediately motioned him to sit back down.

"You want something else? What do you want?" she asked.

Christopher let out a moan—the first noise I had ever heard from him besides his high-pitched squeal.

"You have to use your words, Christopher," she insisted. "Do you want Cheerios?"

I was immediately alert, and my heart began beating faster and faster. I wanted to hear him speak!

His eyes slowly scanned the room. He opened his mouth, and as my eyes widened, he let out a soft and casual, "…Yeah."

"Say please, Christopher. Say please," his mother instructed, clearly not as impressed as I was with this feat of language.

"Puhhh…puhhh…puhhlease. Pulease, mommmm," he said.

I couldn't help it. I put my hand over my mouth, as Linda smiled, stood up, and disappeared in the crowd in search of Cheerios.

10

FOUR WAVES, FOUR BREAKTHROUGHS

"I remember, my friends would ask, 'What's wrong with your brother?' That was hard; once I actually had the words to explain it, things were so much easier, because then other people understood."

Regardless of how fast I drove or how well-planned my route, the trek from South Florida to Tybee Island, the next stop on the 2015 Surf Tour, was an eight-hour drive. So I used those eight hours of road signs and taillights to reflect on the powerful experiences I'd had following this non-profit organization and its group of families on their yearly pilgrimage.

I thought of little blue-eyed Nate Weppner. Though not exactly able to stand on a board yet, he had stopped his previous routine of bolting down the beach once his tiptoes touched sand. Despite his non-verbal label, he knows names—mine included.

Or the adorable Poe twins! Their energy levels were always through the roof, and while they used to fear the bigger swells, this year both had learned to love the extra adrenaline rush.

And Damian, the boy with the photographic memory and the long, surfer-like hair, who now competed in a sport that he first tried on nothing more than a whim—a sport which now defines who he is as a person.

Skye, with those adorable blonde locks, was another person who found identity through Surfers for Autism. And not just that: she also found community and best friends (even potential boyfriends).

Lucas Fuentes, who seemingly grows taller at every event. Even though he only surfs when the water temperature is just right, he makes it look absolutely effortless when gliding across a wave. He makes it all look so easy.

And it wasn't just the children of the families who shared their homes and stories with me. Hundreds of participants did as well, some in meltdown mode, others who couldn't exactly glide across waves like Lucas on their first try, but who were willing enough to get on a board (with a bit of persuasion from Byron, Keith Arnold, and a host of other dedicated volunteers). They return to the sand each time, changed; I've seen the difference with my own eyes.

And just this year, Surfers for Autism—something Don Ryan and others created to help those in need and to function as a support group, a place of acceptance—had in turn helped its founder when he was in need. You couldn't show that script in Hollywood; it would be thrown out for being too cliché.

Through it all, there is an amazing sense of community at the heart of this self-proclaimed "dysfunctional family," which all began with a simple idea: to make a change, to act, to not sit idly.

Heading north, I passed the exit signs for Jupiter, Stuart, Cocoa Beach, Ponce, and Flagler Beach, each in their turn. These names now hold so many memories, not just for me, but for the dozens of families helped by SFA every year.

It's just as Don says: "Each event has a completely different personality from another." Deerfield Beach's celebratory party atmosphere couldn't have been more different from Cocoa Beach's core surfing vibe, or Stuart's challenging conditions. Tybee Island, my current destination, promised to provide us all with the best of Southern hospitality culture.

Passing through Jacksonville, the sky darkened and a torrential downpour began. It reminded me of sitting in a beach chair next to Keith and Christopher at Pass-A-Grille. There, despite the afternoon thunderstorm, no one left: not the volunteers, the participants, or their families. They stayed true to the day and its cause, even though a dry car and quiet hotel room beckoned.

My thoughts shifted once again to that cause that all those people believed in and worked for. I had seen the true effects of autism on a world that operates on an unspoken standard of "NORMAL." A world which fully expects you to walk this way, talk with this way, and not interact with others in a strange manner. I'd seen the stares in restaurants when one of the SFA participants couldn't sit in the booth and instead acted as if it were a small, enjoyable trampoline; the sideways glances when a male participant, 10 or 11 years old, was being strapped into a car seat; the audible gasps when mothers and fathers are seen in hot pursuit of their child in public.

And that's just on the outside. Inside, there's clothes being stripped by a child because of an overwhelmed sensation, heartbreaking stories of the diagnosis process, cracked family portraits. Certainly, with the help of a dedicated parent or two, the glass can be repaired and the focus can return to the smiling faces within the picture frame. But even when the family portrait looks intact, tension still swirls like a hurricane, putting holes in the living room walls.

The night before the Ponce Inlet event, Christine and I stood on a hotel balcony at 1 a.m. along with a few others, overlooking the beach and the empty streets. I listened as Christine recounted her life story, speaking about the goals and aspirations she has for her young twins, who face challenges for which she has yet to determine a solution. Hearing her open up to me, essentially a stranger—both about her family as well as autism—felt as heavy as the rain falling on my windshield as I drove.

I truly felt what it meant to be a part of their little community. Just because it's little, doesn't mean it can't do amazing things; because of SFA coming to town, each city taped off streets, provided helicopters and planes and armored vehicles for a part of the show—even mayors would show up on the sand to present yet another key from yet another city—all in support of every SFA family, new or tenured. I remember Don telling me multiple times that city governments have actually come to him in hopes of starting an SFA event in their community.

The same goes for the volunteers, filling the ranks at each event. The stories I'd heard from volunteers after a full event day showed me that they get as much out of it as the families and the participants. As with the families, the volunteers have become like friends to me.

Especially Byron. When I crossed the state line into Georgia, and the rain subsided, I stopped outside of Byron's house, located within the urban sprawl of Savannah. He greeted me with a bear hug and showed me into his home, the interior of which resembled a surf shop: clothes, posters, and designs pointed to all things beach culture.

We spent the rest of the night out in proper pub-crawl form. In bar after bar, we caught each other up on past happenings and discussed what the following day's conditions were forecasted to look like, only stopping our conversation to dance with strangers in strobe-lit rooms.

Looking out from the Arnold's family tent the next morning, the sky above Tybee Island looked gray. A light drizzle dampened the sand, and the water presented a wholly un-surfable shore break wave. It was a stark contrast to the clear blue and rolling water the Tour had seen at its previous stops in South Florida.

The combination of the long drive, dancing all night, and having only a few hours of sleep proved to be the perfect cocktail of exhaustion that even now ran through my veins. But when we woke up, Byron was already moving quickly and purposefully as he packed the car, so I had to do the same.

My attention shifted at the sound of a beautiful, resounding voice magnificently singing the National Anthem to kick off the event. Deafening applause followed, and as I peered my head out of the tent for a better view, it was evident that the singer, a young woman with Down syndrome, couldn't stop blushing in front of the roughly 200 onlookers giving her a well-deserved 15 seconds of fame.

As Christopher and Keith emerged from the tent to start greeting the other SFA frequents, I had a chance to catch up with Linda.

"I've been meaning to ask you about Christopher's therapy," I began. "What has that been like for him?"

"It's intensive integration; all his behavior therapy's intensive," she responded. "There were times when he was out of control—he could flip a table at a restaurant. He wouldn't be able to communicate, and you could tell it was frustrating for him. I think I've said this before, but the strange thing is he's a saint in church. The whole Mass, he kneels; even if you don't have a kneeler, he kneels on the ground. Church has always been something that's there for him, with his disability."

"How much money have you guys spent on his therapy, do you think?" I asked, unsure of how the question would be received.

"Depends on insurance," she answered easily. "I'd say…$20,000 out of pocket so far. When Christopher was a preemie, they didn't expect him to do much. But medication can be upwards of $250, and the insurance won't pay for his therapies. Plus, there's blood work involved…"

I was floored. It wasn't enough for autism to provide its own challenges—apparently it had to be expensive, too.

"In the beginning it was hard," said Miranda Fuentes, standing in the volunteer chute, awaiting another volunteer for the third session of the day. "But now, working with these kids, I've gotten used to it."

Throughout the Tour, I had heard a lot about the dynamic between parents and children with autism. Now I wanted to see if it was different sibling to sibling.

"I have to imagine it was hard for you when Lucas was first diagnosed. You weren't too old when it happened, right?" I asked, as the noises of laughter and spirited conversation rose and fell, in complete defiance of the gloomy gray sky.

"Now that I'm older, it makes more sense," she replied. "I don't think I officially knew until I was maybe 7 or 8, and then I started SFA at 9.

"I remember, my friends would ask, 'What's wrong with your brother?' That was hard; once I actually had the words to explain it, things were so much easier, because then other people understood.

"Some people would still give him dirty looks, though. Like, a year ago, we were somewhere and a tantrum happened and a passerby made some comment, and I just said, 'Do you want to take a picture? What's the problem?!' I'm more understanding of it now."

Suddenly, I heard a voice calling, "Team leader, I need a team leader! Miranda!" Monica Valdez was standing nearby, eyes searching for Miranda.

Miranda immediately headed off to answer the call, emerging from the chutes a few moments later with a small, quiet boy in tow. After I watched Miranda begin her "Up, Up, Up" mantra, I weaved through the packed crowd until I spotted Michele standing with Joe, Monica's soon-to-be husband. Just as integral to these events as Monica, Joe serves as timekeeper and coordinator down at the waterline at every event.

He and Monica first met at an SFA event, as it happens—and they're not the only ones. Byron proposed to his wife during an event the previous year, and according to Kim Ryan, there had been two other proposals during event days in the past.

Picking out Nate in the lineup, I kept my eyes on him as a team of volunteers pushed him out on flat water, simulating a wave like at the Pass-a-Grille event. He popped to his knees, and there he stayed until he reached the sand, where he waited to be taken out again.

"Oh, I want him to stand so bad," said Michele, cold water biting at our ankles.

No one could have guessed what the day held in store for Nate that day.

To be honest, the setting didn't seem right for new victories and breakthroughs. You'd expect to see the walls crumble on a perfect, blue-sky day, like we'd had at Jupiter or Cocoa Beach; or on a day where the surf was perfect, like Ponce Inlet and Flagler Beach; or even at a big event where the energy on the beach is electric, like at Deerfield Beach.

But no, it would be at gray, chilly Tybee Island. And it all began in the Arnold's tent.

"You want to surf again, Christopher?" I asked, stepping into their family tent after bidding Michele goodbye. I had hoped to have a chance for more conversation with Christopher, after seeing the speech barrier shake at breakfast.

"He's talking to you, Christopher," said Linda casually, who remained focused on her phone.

Silently I was begging for Christopher to say something, anything. So I thought up something simple that he might like: "Christopher? You want to surf again?"

Then it happened. "Ya....yaaaa!" he blurted out with a huge smile.

I didn't care how much it might hurt later. Nothing was stopping my smile.

I arrived at the cold waterline a few minutes later, as I heard Monica say in a booming voice, "I need a master volunteer! Master Volunteer... Byron!"

Seconds later, Byron flew by. It was almost enough to give me déjà vu from Deerfield Beach: a large boy was in full meltdown mode near the participant chute, utterly uncontrollable and kicking gray sand in every direction, belting out cries and moans and slurs.

After a heavy dose of coaxing, Byron and three other strapping volunteers were able to walk with the large boy, who looked to be 14 or 15, towards the waterline and into the cold ocean. His wails only grew louder and louder, making the reggae beats seem like a distant whistling. Finally, they persuaded the boy to lay on the board. Byron sat behind him, holding the boy from slipping off. He continued to fight every inch of the process, only relenting when his energy levels diminished halfway through the heat.

At the same time, close to the pier located just north of the contest site, Christopher glided across the surface of the ocean, his eyes (and mouth) wide open the whole time. I noticed that Christopher and Nate were kindred spirits: both favored belly rides and female volunteers.

When the heat ended, I searched for Byron and his team, noticing the tremendous wailing was gone. In its place was only the calming sound of water washing at the soft sand.

When I finally spotted Byron, he was still holding the boy on the board. His hands were submerged in the sea, as though trying to draw the stillness of the water through himself and into his participant.

Once again, the team pushed the duo toward shore, simulating a wave, where a cheer section awaited.

The boy walked out of the water on his own power, saltwater having replaced his tears.

Noticing participants already joining up with volunteers, Byron swiveled his head in my direction and nodded. I quickly exchanged my rain jacket for a rash guard and made my way down to the waterline, wading out into the sea with Byron. I took a look at his new participant: the adorable crisscross applesauce girl from Deerfield Beach. Her bright smile completely belied her heartbreaking disability.

"We have to get her to stand," I said to Byron as we pulled her into the salty sea. She shivered but remained smiling. "She didn't do it in Deerfield, but I know she can. She's had a ton of reps by now."

But even though we tried to warm her up by running her and the board to shore, she remained on her belly, clinging to Byron's massive biceps any chance she could. We sat for a few quiet minutes, bobbing in the sea until Byron decided to try again.

This time, something clicked.

He began the chant of "Up, Up, Up," as we rushed her toward the sand. Suddenly, she raised up off her belly, placed her hands and knees shoulder and hip width apart, and without using Byron or me for support, she rose from her hips—rose and rose to a full standing position, her brain firing too fast and on too many cylinders for her mouth to keep up.

Her mother on shore was applauding deliriously, and it felt as if Byron and I had been a part of something special: a feeling that was powerful enough to make a mother tear up over how proud she was of her daughter.

After more simulated waves and a hug and thank you from her loving mother, we knew the next heat would be the last of the day. The beach had thinned, and the prospect of a warm shower was sounding more and more appealing.

Then Michele appeared, pulling Nate along behind her. It was clear, even from a distance, that he was in full meltdown mode.

She looked at Byron, who immediately ran onto the shore and whisked Nate away, back towards the board I was holding.

Nate's eyes were red. His body looked tense, and he seemed uncomfortable in his own skin. Byron placed him on the board and, as we started to push Nate out to sea, he jumped into the drink, inadvertently hitting Byron.

"Did he just kick you in the nuts?" yelled Michele from the beach, her voice carrying the 15 yards.

"Yeah! Yeah he did!" came the tender reply.

Nate seemed committed to spending more time in the sea than on the board, but Byron was taking it easy. "Let him do his thing," he advised.

While I trailed him, Nate doggie-paddled a few yards towards the horizon, before turning back toward Byron and the other volunteer teams, where he proceeded to start circling us and the board.

When Byron hoisted him back onto the foam board, everything had changed. Nate was smiling. His blue eyes were no longer distraught, and his body looked excited, not stressed. Saltwater and gleeful noises dribbled out of his lips. He just looked happy.

"We're gonna get you up, Nate, we're gonna get you up!" Byron encouraged.

Standing in the flat sea, he began chanting and Nate popped to his knees with ease, just like he had done at so many other SFA events throughout the years.

We began to give the board momentum.

"Here we go, we're gonna get up, Nate! Let's go! Up, Up, Up!"

In a full sprint, we pushed the board to shore. From his knees, Nate slowly rose up, putting one foot flat on the board before dropping back to his knees.

We ran the board to the beach twice with the same results, but Byron showed no signs of quitting.

"Let's go, Nate, we're not giving up! Keep trying!"

Then, on the next push, it happened. Nate once again slightly rose, putting one foot flat on the board, followed with his next foot…and rose to a full stand.

Byron let out a shocked gasp. We were both speechless. The sight re-energized us, and we sped even faster towards the shoreline. Michele had her hand covering her mouth, looking as though she were trying to hold back the flood.

"Nate! Yeah! Yeah, Nate, yeah! You did it! You're standing!" Byron cried.

Nate instantly knew he had accomplished something incredible: he belted out noises of joy, laughing and flapping his hands as a smile spread across his face. Once we reached the shore, he looked down at the sea from his new point of view and jumped back in.

"Again, Nate! Let's get you standing again!" Byron urged.

After we pushed him back out in the sea, now crowded with other participants and volunteers, Nate again rose to his feet, as if it were the easiest thing in the world, all the while laughing, oooooohing, and ahhhhhhing.

About 10 minutes later, as Michele wrapped her smiling son in a towel onshore, the only thing she could say was a soft, "Thank you, thank you, thank you…"

11
THE LAST WAVE

"One of the things we did not foresee when we started this was how it would affect more than just the participants that surf. Friendships are made, siblings can hang out together and share feelings. Parents have someone else to talk to who understands. Volunteers have life-changing experiences. Isn't that the whole point?"

A bigail Maass may be diagnosed with nonverbal autism, but that doesn't mean she doesn't have a specific taste in music. It was 8 a.m., the day before the Surf Tour stop in Jacksonville Beach, when faint strains of Chumbawamba's 90's classic "Tubthumping" (you know the one: "I get knocked down, but I get up again...") reached my ears, coming through the radio in the Maass' car.

"Abigail must not like this song right now..." I thought. And sure enough, while we waited in the driveway for her husband, Priscilla changed the radio station and John Legend's "All of Me" poured through the SUV speakers. Immediately, Abigail began belting out a jumble of consonants and vowels, bouncing up and down in her car seat.

"So she likes John Legend and Top 40?" I wondered out loud.

Asa slid into the passenger seat, apologizing for keeping everyone waiting, and we headed out of the subdivision towards Abigail's school.

I was spending the day before the SFA event with the Maass family. Given my goal of understanding autism more, Asa and Priscilla warmly invited me to visit Abigail's school. I instantly agreed, excited to talk with them, and take advantage of their incredible wisdom and openness on the subject of their daughter's autism.

The change in weather and scenery was striking. Jacksonville exhibited few of the classic Floridian qualities: the sky looked cloudy and overcast, but there was a cool breeze. More clothing was required than the average Florida t-shirt, shorts, and sandals, and instead of swamps or beaches, the landscape was dotted with pine trees, buildings, and all-purpose suburbia.

By the time we reached the interstate, the conversation had turned to common topics—namely, SFA.

"It has to be the biggest life changing event," said Asa, his eyes trained on his iPhone as he edited a video to show Abigail's teachers her progress with brushing her teeth. "You'll hear that from Don and others, too. It's not just the surfing, either; it's all-encompassing."

Entering Abigail's two-story brick school building, nestled in a quiet area just off the interstate, the love the teachers had for their students was palpable. The instructors all stood near their classroom doors, welcoming children on this Friday morning like they were their own children.

"The whole school is solely for autism," said Priscilla, after we said our goodbyes and got back onto the interstate. "Out of 23 kids in the school, only five or six are girls."

"Mathematically, it makes sense," said Asa, referring to the notion that more boys are diagnosed on the autism spectrum than girls. In fact, boys are nearly five times more likely than girls to have autism.[1]

"When was her diagnosis?" I asked. "At age two, or maybe a bit after?"

"Well, the diagnosis was infantile autism," said Priscilla, pausing to change lanes. "Around twelve months, we knew something wasn't right, but we didn't know what. At sixteen months we took her to the Medical University in Charleston, and at age two they diagnosed her with infantile autism.

"We received this ten-page report. They'd had five different specialists evaluate her for eight hours, and there was a lot to go through. They gave us a plan of action, though at that point Abigail had already been receiving therapy—she had no speech ability at all. The diagnosis was very much, 'This is what it is and this is what you need to do.' We were frustrated and angry—still are, at times."

"Like I said, we already knew *something* was off," continued Asa. "This just gave her a label. But it was definitely not a shock. But when you have it on paper…it's different. We still cried about it, even knowing to expect bad news. It still hurt, and there's that level of denial that lingered…but there's always a little bit of hope. We sat down and thought about it and realized that, just because she has something on paper, nothing had changed. She didn't *become* autistic once she got the diagnosis; it was already there. She was the same kid and, when I realized that, nothing really changed."

"Right," I said, nodding.

"That said, our faith in general has been changed drastically," said Asa.

"It's made us question," Priscilla clarified. "And that's terrible; you shouldn't do that, I know, but…it's like someone who gets a diagnosis of cancer. How can you not question it? Abigail is so pure, and yet she's been diagnosed with autism," said Priscilla.

"I was in Bible College Seminary to be a preacher," Asa continued. "And I very closely followed every utterance and word of Scripture. I'm not saying that Abigail's diagnosis made me doubt my belief in a higher power…but it got me thinking enough to start evaluating exactly what I *did* believe in. I'm a logical person. It's not logical that all these things the Bible talks about…would a loving and just God allow for an angel like Abigail to have to deal with this every day? What did we do that we have to deal with this in our lives?" His voice trailed off.

I simply didn't know what to say, so I stayed silent, continuing to listen.

Then he said, "But it's small-minded to put God into a box like that."

His voice was stern but calm.

"He's not a puppet master controlling the little-bitty aspects of our lives. I have a hard time believing everything happened by accident. In light of everything that works so perfectly and in harmony together, the only thing I see that screws up the way the world works is the human factor.

"I'm not saying there aren't definite blessings: our son Isaiah is going to be an amazing person. And a lot of what has shaped him is his sister's disability. He's going to become an amazing adult. And our marriage is certainly stronger because of it," he added, looking at Priscilla. "We're better people because of it, we look at the world differently. We're more open minded, we know what unconditional love is."

"How *does* Isaiah view his sister's disability?" I asked. "I know that he helps out volunteering at SFA events."

"I'm sure that, internally, there's some resentment there. But there's also a strong desire to nurture," Asa replied. "They say that if everyone were to throw their problems into one pile, you'd take one look at everyone else's issues and pull your own right back out. Everyone has something they have to handle in their lifetime."

"We can't say we've seen anger or anything outwardly," interjected Priscilla. "He's just as much a caregiver as he is a sibling to Abigail. Sure, he wants to hang out with adults more than his peers. But I was an only child, and that's how I was."

"It's matured him; God knows he's ten years beyond his age. He does do kid stuff, but he's very mature. It's difficult for him to relate to his peers," said Asa.

"But we make it a point to do his things, too," added Priscilla.

"He fully understands that a lot of the time we spend on Abigail isn't 'Abigail-time,'" Asa said. "It's 'autism time.' We have to do it, because of autism. We've had that discussion, too: how, without autism, Abigail would be completely different.

"Some people ask us, 'Would you want to take the autism away?' And it's hard to say, because then Abigail wouldn't be Abigail. You see how smart she is; her whole personality has to do with autism."

"It would take away her purity," said Asa. "She doesn't lie. She doesn't intentionally hurt your feelings, she's free of natural born sin, to put it Biblically."

"Jacksonville is getting better in terms of special needs services, too. North Carolina was terrible, and in Virginia we'd have to drive hours to get any services, because we lived in a small town."

"I've asked this of a few people, because it seems like a lot of SFA families on the beach consist of single moms," I said. "It's probably not statistically proven, but how much stress *does* autism put on a marriage?"

"There was a point, right after we had Abigail, where we didn't go out at all," Asa admitted. "Our longest stint was almost two years doing nothing, and I mean *nothing*. Leaving the house together without children did not occur for almost two years."

I was shocked. I knew this was by no means exclusive to the Maass'—I'm sure many parents with children on the autism spectrum have experienced this inability to go out for months, perhaps even years on end. But to hear it put so plainly really put it in perspective.

He continued: "It was hard, but we had no options for babysitters. And it gets to you, it does; every day you're going home and having to shoulder that level of responsibly. Even as an adult, it wears you down."

"The divorce rate *is* very high," Priscilla agreed. "So we've taken a different approach and worked as a team. There are some things Asa does better with Abigail and some things I do better with her."

"I'm totally guessing here, but I'll bet a lot of dads don't want to be involved in all-day school, or therapy day after day. It starts off that way, and it just gets worse as time goes on," added Asa. "The less you know about autism, the less you're capable of providing care for your child. I'm sure that leads to a lot of fights, which eventually leads to that 85 percent divorce rate you hear tossed around" (a number which Michele Weppner had briefed me on earlier in the Surf Tour).

"We've both decided we could never do this by ourselves. We're stuck with each other anyway," Priscilla said, smiling at her husband.

"You mourn often," said Asa. "You really do. You think the grief process is linear, but you find yourself going back to things that are out of order. You mourn the death of those dreams, those things you wanted for your child."

I kept listening.

"Then your goals change," Asa said. "There are new goals to work toward. If you were to ask us, 'Did you ever think Abigail would ever talk?' In our heart of hearts, even though we still have hope, it's easier for us to say no. It's easier for us to say, 'Probably not.' She'll probably never talk, but then you meet people, like one of Abigail's classmates, who's a year or two older, and now she's saying hello to everyone."

"You see stuff like that and you think, 'Maybe...'" said Priscilla. "But I think we've come to a point where we're okay if Abigail doesn't talk."

"The dreams change. I don't want to say it's gone, because that's morbid; but it's changed. Now it's learning effective communication."

"Do you still think about walking her down the aisle and such?" I asked Asa.

"Absolutely," he affirmed. "I do hope some dude marries her and takes her away," he added, laughing.

"We joke about that!" Priscilla agreed. "She's pretty, and she has more than just that going for her! We used to cry a lot, now we laugh a lot."

"You do laugh, at least to keep from crying," said Asa. "You find the humor in situations. Things like when Abigail gets out of her PJs and before you know it, she's pooped. We'll be texting each other while I'm at work and she's saying, 'The shit has hit the fan.' And literally, there is shit on the fan."

Priscilla nodded. "I went out with some girlfriends recently. I came home, I had this awful hangover, and Abigail decided to smear poop on the wall the next morning. So I'm sweating alcohol, and Asa says, 'I'll take care of this.'"

"Long and short is, we're together almost every day, between the kids and working. We do all of that together, so we might as well like each other."

"Plus, we've become pretty public figures within Abigail's school and Isaiah's group of friends," remarked Asa. "People follow our lives on Facebook, all because of autism."

"We just want to show that if you're a new family and you get the diagnosis, it's not the end of the world," said Priscilla. "Yeah, it sucks. Like today: I know we have to go home and pack for SFA and it's going to be so hard to pack with Abigail there. A typical ten-year-old, you should be able to let them hang out while you're packing, but not with autism. It's the little things like that where, if you dwell on them, it makes things that much harder. People say, 'I don't know how you do it.' And I say, 'It's your kid. It's not like you have a choice.'"

"You guys have been attending SFA events for years," I said, moving on to the next subject. "Has it become a form of therapy for Abigail? Or is it more of a community? Or both?"

"Would you say there's therapeutic benefits, Asa?" asked Priscilla.

"Some," he replied. "Abigail is different at the beach than anywhere else. In the beginning of our time at SFA, she loved surfing; she got right on the board and did it. Then she went through a period where she wasn't really into it, or wasn't excited until some specific volunteers started working with her. Eventually she got more into the surfing part. And in that aspect, yes, it's therapeutic."

Priscilla then commented on a common narrative I'd heard at events: SFA *wasn't* just for the participants.

"I have girlfriends and stuff, but I grew up on a military base removed from everything," said Priscilla. "So our SFA friends…these are people I can call and tell them anything. They get it. They don't judge. We don't have a job to make friends. There's very little personal time with autism. We just don't have the opportunity to have that in our lives, honestly. For me, that's why I look forward to SFA events—because of the family aspect of it. Isaiah has the opportunity to have friends and siblings like Miranda Fuentes, who share a common goal. I think that's why I look forward to it."

"Isaiah loves the service, the volunteering aspect," Asa said. "It gives him a high, you can tell. He'll say, 'Dad, make sure I get up.' He wants to get up at 5:30 a.m. to help with set-up. That's his thing, and that's without us telling him."

Priscilla's office is, more or less, the driver's seat in the family SUV. She spends most weekdays driving between Isaiah and Abigail's schools, their two-story house, and their shop.

Priscilla and Asa opened a motorcycle, ATV, and small engine repair shop, a decision which had more to do with Abigail's needs than anything. Owning their own business afforded them the opportunity to set their own schedule and work around Abigail's therapy sessions.

After spending the remainder of the cool morning in their store, filled door to door with ATVs, lawnmowers, motorcycles, and other pieces of equipment that needed repair, we ventured back to Abigail's school for pick-up.

Asa and Priscilla had agreed to provide an interview about the benefits of ABA therapy at Abigail's school, a testimonial that the school could later show to other parents. Since I was still new to ABA and other forms of therapy, I hoped their testimonial would give me some insight into the therapy process.

Upon arriving, we peered into Abigail's classroom before being led to a bench behind the building by a faculty member, who greeted us warmly. The sky had remained overcast and the sea felt hundreds of miles away. The air felt like fall.

Priscilla and Asa were set up in front of a camera, and told to start whenever they were ready.

"We have a daughter, Abigail, who is ten years old," Priscilla began. "She's been doing ABA for four years now."

Asa took over, saying, "She's severely autistic, diagnosed with infantile autism with a cognitive level of a 10–12-month-old. She's nonverbal. We're working on potty training, to give you an idea of the level she is at. Early on, the struggle we faced was not knowing how to incorporate what she was learning at therapy into our daily life. We had to train ourselves, learning what Abigail was doing and being able to apply that in our home setting.

"We could see a clear difference," he continued. "Abigail could operate a zipper better, could manipulate Velcro or stack blocks. Just this morning I was able to take some of the principles I learned from ABA and, after being trained by Abigail's therapist, help her brush her teeth. She's gone from being completely resistant, not allowing a toothbrush in her mouth at all, to now putting it in her own mouth. We're able to apply what we learned and collaborate with her teachers and therapists. It's a day-to-day thing, not a 30 minutes a day, twice-a-week therapy. It turns into a lifestyle."

"Our son Isaiah implements the things he sees. He sits in on therapies, so everyone is on the same page," Priscilla resumed. "We've seen more progress with ABA in a year than we did with any other therapy over a period of five years. I don't think it would be as beneficial if we weren't involved or failed to follow through with the 'technical' information the therapist taught us."

"One concern with other therapies is that, as parents, we didn't have a say-so until everything was already written or done and signed off," said Asa. "We're not doctors, therapists, or teachers. We don't know the direction her therapy needs to go in. We are trusting strangers with her future and her education.

"But, with a collaboration, it's different because we have a say in things. And it's daily, so it does build your relationship with the therapists, with the teachers. And you are so much more trusting with their plans for your child's future."

"The biggest thing I see that is different in ABA is that it's ongoing. It can change day to day," said Priscilla. "Everybody is open to things; that's what makes it nice."

"We get daily updates, too, and we can make little adjustments," added Asa. "We've sent in photos, things we're trying at home, and we get emails back with recommendations. It's refreshing to have professionals take our opinion and run with it."

Finally, Asa spoke about his thoughts on the long-term effects of ABA. "The tools we've been given by these therapists and by the teachers have prepared us for the future. We don't feel like we're going at this alone. We're better equipped to face Abigail's future, and we feel like we have the tools we need to be successful. We're not relying on other people, funding, or even insurance to improve Abigail's future.

"And at the end of the day, this is all to prepare her for her future."

After my day with the Maass', I headed in the direction of the SFA-sponsored hotel. I knew I had the correct address from the moment I entered the parking lot: hordes of SUVs with blue and white SFA bumper stickers lined the lot, while a steady flow of familiar faces streamed from their cars into the hotel.

I headed towards where I heard the most noise, namely the pool. As soon as I arrived, one thing was immediately clear: Nate Weppner seemingly had a future in track and field.

There was a battle raging in his big blue eyes—eyes reflecting a pool teeming with children and teenagers, some of who would be participating in the following morning's last stop on the Atlantic coast of the Surf Tour.

"Nate, listen to me. Do not jump in, you have all of your clothes on," said Michele, who had one hand interlaced with his and the other holding her purse. "You can surf tomorrow morning."

I'd experienced this scene many times in the Weppner's backyard; even though Nate was fully clothed, he would frequently jump in their pool at a moment's notice. Needless to say, I was keeping a wary eye on Nate, curious to see what would happen next.

Nate's eyes darted toward the beach access gate, then back to the pool, then at the waterfall standing at the far end of the area. He pulled at his shirt, his body growing more tense.

Suddenly, he wrestled free of his mother's grip and took off in a mad dash.

"Nate!" Michele pleaded.

Her plaintive call was met only with the sound of suddenly displaced water, which erupted over our feet and the slippery concrete. Michele was hot on his trail, darting to each corner of the pool as Nate paddled from one end to the other, having a blast the whole time. Michele only slowed down once to yell in the direction of another SFA frequent flier, sitting on the opposite side of the pool, "He's overstimulated!"

For all the aggravation, Nate relished in the moment, as Kami and her daughter Skye, Tracy and her son Damian, Don and Kim Ryan, the Fuentes clan, and Christine and Evan Poe all joined us by the pool for family-like conversation.

Heading back after a beachside dinner at the hotel café with the core SFA members, we stepped out of the elevator and into a full-blown party. The air was loud, and rows of sandaled feet from members of the SFA family blocked any attempt to walk through the hallway. At least the feet were easier to step over than the enormous cooler, filled to the brim with "liquid courage," which dominated the center of the scene.

The remainder of that Friday night was a blur of conversations, mostly centered around examining the various costumes that families had purchased for the Western-themed afterparty set to take place after the following day's SFA event (a combination wrap-up party and birthday celebration for Don Ryan).

As the conversation finally began to slow, the hotel door that Christine Poe was leaning up against slowly opened, and out came Michele and Nate. He looked tired and sluggish but seemed to quickly tap into the electric atmosphere, recharging up to full power in the blink of an eye. No more than a minute later, he was hopping and pacing back and forth through the rows of feet, before abruptly dashing to the other end of the hallway, a stretch of about 20 or 30 yards. Michele jumped up, took a lighting fast step, then stopped.

"Is that a dead end?" she asked.

"Yeah, I think so," said Byron in a serious tone. The group nodded in agreement; this sort of awareness was second nature to them at this point.

So the conversations continued, as Nate reached the end of the hallway, stopped, turned around, and sprinted back our way. Everyone rapidly pulled up their feet to avoid being trampled, which was all well and good, until he reached the other end and disappeared behind a wall, followed by the unmistakable sound of a door being opened.

"The fire escape!" Michele screamed, and went off like a shot, returning a few minutes later with a grinning Nate in tow.

"He's not bothering anyone, so let's get all that energy out," she said tiredly, shrugging her shoulders and letting him continue running through the hallway as, automatically, the sitting crowd shifted to block his path towards the fire escape.

They're all old hands at that sort of thing by now.

When Byron and I left our hotel room the following morning for the Jacksonville event, the hallway that had been loud with chatter the night before was empty. We got down to the lobby and found a few SFA volunteers already wandering the hallway, looking for coffee. We followed the foot traffic out of the lobby, onto the pool deck that Nate took advantage of the night before, and then walked out to the dark sea.

The conditions looked rough, to the say the least: shoulder-high onshore swell was pounding the sand in a chaotic manner. It shot up past the high tide line and into the mangroves, the last line of defense between the sea and the hotel. There was hardly a single patch of dry sand to stand on, and the breeze felt cold and cutting.

"We had a blood moon last night, along with an extreme high tide," Don informed everyone over the speaker half an hour later, as the beach started getting more crowded and the sun began to rise above the horizon. "We're waiting for the tide to go back out. In about an hour from now, we're going to have 100 yards of sand right here. And if you're an exhibitor, don't worry; we're going to give you the most beautiful exhibition area you've ever seen." And just as Don predicted, the tide receded in time for the event, and by the time the sun had fully burst out of the water, the beach looked entirely different.

After the volunteer instruction meeting, the first heat took to the water. The first round was loaded with SFA frequent fliers: Skye, Damian, and Christopher all confronted the large, disorganized swell head-on—literally. Each showed their growing skill in adapting to the swell, and within a few minutes of the start of the heat, all three had somehow managed to surf the large waves to shore.

"Last year at this event, we were surfing in the pouring rain," Kami Lambert remarked as we watched Skye roll in on the avalanching whitewash.

"Really?" I asked, surprised.

She nodded. "But if you looked at Facebook the following week, you'd see everyone saying this was the best event ever. You see these clouds behind us?" She pointed. "Watch, Skye is going to ask if it's going to storm. A few years ago, it thundered here, and she ran all the way back into the hotel. She hates storms."

We watched Skye pop up again, slide down the face of a wave and nosedive. On the next wave, she placed her feet farther back on the board and, after making the drop, rode until she hit sand, her grin clearly evident. She started scanning the beach, searching for her mother, and as soon as she spotted her, Skye's hand rose towards the dark clouds.

"It's okay, trust Mr. Don!" Kami yelled, as we both laughed.

But when Abigail ventured out to sea, protected by a life-jacketed team of volunteers, it was obvious just how challenging the conditions really were. The volunteers were careful not to push her onto the largest waves, which would crash moments after they appeared into explosions of whitewash. Instead, they waited for less intimidating waves to come through before giving her a push towards shore, where her parents stood anxiously watching.

Despite the conditions, however, Abigail looked at peace and comfortable. "The ocean is the one and only place that Abigail is always happy," Asa explained. "Just like anyone else, she has bad days and can be in bad moods. But when she's on a surfboard, her mood is always happy and content."

After watching Abigail's surf sessions, I joined forces with a 40-something-year-old volunteer to push Evan into the swell, which had decreased in size since mid-morning with the changing of the tides. From the sea, the entire event scene took on a different feel. The air was much quieter, and you could see how expansive the beach party truly was.

As each wave pushed through in close proximity, Evan flipped his head back towards the sea to size up the surf. And though a third of the waves we pushed him on resulted in a wipeout, given the difficult conditions, we kept encouraging him. "Sit farther back on your board! You're too close to the nose."

The 10-year-old rallied, a model of calm composure amidst the chaos of the sea. He took the last two waves to the beach, where Christine awaited him with camera phone in hand.

"The other volunteer," she asked after we all took a photo, with Evan sitting on my back. "Do you know who he was?"

"No," I replied, "but he was really good with Evan."

"He drove down here just for Evan," she informed me. "I think he's from somewhere in Georgia. The two met at an event a while ago. How sweet is that?"

"Amazing!" I said.

As the mother and son duo turned back towards the alleyway of tents, I spotted Tracy at the waterline, which was perfect, as I had a burning question I needed to ask her.

"Hey!" I called, jogging up. "I meant to ask earlier. How was Damian's competition? I heard he got first at a recent Special Olympics contest!"

"The volunteers let him paddle into his own waves!" she reported happily. "He's getting so much stronger."

She started to go into the details of the competition, when suddenly her figure exploded with energy, as if she was paddling for a wave herself. Eyes fixed out to sea, she loudly instructed, "Up, Up, Up! Use your balance, Damian! All the way to the beach! Good job!"

The only times I've seen Don Ryan alone have been before and after SFA events, when he is either setting up or tearing down. That's why it was so surprising to see him standing alone in the main SFA tent as the sun climbed higher and higher over Jacksonville Beach.

I immediately seized my opportunity. "You've been to—and put on—so many of these events. How do you keep them new and exciting?" I asked. "How do you avoid them becoming routine?"

His eyes were so focused on me that I felt like the only person on the beach. "I don't allow it to," he replied. "Jobs get routine, and with routine comes monotony. I don't *have* to do all of this, because I was chosen for this. I take that responsibility very seriously, and so I don't allow it to be routine.

"I have a template for the way everything works," he continued to explain, "because it has to be duplicated market to market and I can't have any randomness. These events are too big and too important to be random. And I follow that template to the letter, market to market.

"But each of these events has their own personality, too; I've said that before. Each event has different challenges—like this morning, with us not being able to set up on time. But I plan; I do the math. Inch by inch, on where the tide would be in case we had to set up a little bit later. When you create a space that is free of judgment, an example of inclusion at the highest level…people will show up. The key to being successful is consistency. Provide the same positive experience over and over at each host location."

"The level of community support SFA receives seems unprecedented," I remarked, remembering the scene in the Stuart court house as Don accepted the key to the city on behalf of SFA. "Why have you guys been able to get so much support? Is it the cause, or the work of the co-founders?"

"There's a number of reasons," Don replied, thinking. "I would like to think that the main reason is that each community, when provided the opportunity to support, host, and entertain their special needs population, is willing to take advantage of it. The people have shown that there is a need for our program; I'm not surprised that the community feels they almost have an obligation to respond.

"There is also an understanding that there is no agenda in our events. Neither myself nor my organization has anything to gain by being here. By which I mean, these events are free and open to the public; they are not fundraisers. So communities can feel confident that we are going to produce a first-class, grand scale event that is safe and fun for the entire community.

"Plus, these events are also revenue generators. These events see attendance, not in the hundreds, but in the thousands. That's people in hotels, restaurant seats, and in retail businesses. Everyone wins."

"You've seen the participants grow up year by year," I asked, his eyes still glued to mine, momentarily ignoring the roar at the waterline. "What does that mean to you?"

"For me…to know with certainty that you played even a small part in the growth and progression of an individual with special needs is unfathomable. And I mean significant progression—neurological, psychological, social, and physical. To watch my kids grow and excel in all of these areas…it's incredibly gratifying. It has been worth every challenge faced to create and grow this foundation.

"And then there are the volunteers," he continued. "You want to talk about moving? To witness countless teens and even pre-teen children, who began volunteering to fulfill some scholastic requirement, and who are now in college seeking degrees as special needs educators, therapists, and caregivers…is a feeling that cannot be described. Because of this foundation, these kids have the capacity to change the world."

By dinner, the hotel restaurant, which featured a small wooden deck overlooking a beach crowded with tables, looked like the movie set of a Western film. Sunburnt families trickled in: the Poes, the Maass', the Arnolds, Fuentes, Tracy and Damian, Michele and Nate, Skye and Kami, and more.

The atmosphere was laid back…at least, until dinner finished. That's when the DJ arrived, setting up in a corner of the restaurant, a keg was wheeled out, and Don and Kim Ryan appeared in full cowboy regalia. The party fire was lit.

For the next hour and a half, a group of 20 to 30 SFA frequent fliers, brought together by the bonds of autism, surfing, and the beach lifestyle, danced hand in hand through different eras and genres of music, nearly cracking the wooden dance floor beneath their feet.

There were roaring conga lines, with Miranda in the lead; Priscilla Maass, Laura Fuentes, Byron, Christine Poe, and other volunteers shook their hips and heads to rap hits; Don, along with Kami Lambert, bellowed out every word to Def Leppard's "Pour Some Sugar on Me."

Then, once the party had reached a critical mass of noise (and running time), the music stopped; because of the late hour, the hotel had called the party quits.

Voiceless, sunburnt and exhausted, I followed the families as we ebbed out of the restaurant and back into the quiet hotel corridors.

The faint noise of the crowd, audible even from the elevator, turned into a roar as soon as I reached the first floor the next morning. The excited vibe within the breakfast area, filled with familiar faces, felt more like of a pick-me-up than the best cup of coffee.

Ethan and Evan Poe couldn't keep still while eating; an animated Don Ryan was speaking with family members; Christopher Arnold was shoveling food in his mouth while maintaining a radiant smile; and Abigail Maass moaned excitedly as breakfast was set before her.

After an hour of trading stories from the previous day, stories borne from salt, sea-foam, and the joy of success, the tables began to empty one by one. Families filled the lobby, ready to venture home, where a new week of work and therapy for their children awaited them.

With suitcases in tow, all said their goodbyes to participants and families alike, hugging each other and promising, "See you at the next event!"

EPILOGUE

The hotel lobby in Jacksonville Beach is the last memory of my years with the SFA family. Fittingly, my journey ended at the same event where it had started, years before.

Even though there were two more stops left on the 2015 Tour—Naples and Ft Myers, two flat-water events on the Gulf of Mexico that take on a relaxed vibe, along with an annual and unforgettable Halloween party—I left.

I left because a few weeks prior to the Jacksonville event, an offer came my way that I couldn't turn down—an offer to work for a surf magazine in Hawaii.

Although the opportunity seemed like a no brainer, I decided to ask some of those closest to me for advice, which happened to be families involved with SFA.

Christine Poe said to "Follow my gut." Michele Weppner, holding Nate's hand all the while, reiterated how truly important it was to do what I wanted to do while still in my twenties. Linda Arnold, while lathering Christopher in sunscreen, smiled and said that it would all work out. Byron said I should definitely move, and that he'd love to come visit.

I also felt I had achieved my goal: I had discovered what motivates each family to embark on the Surf Tour and I'd seen how surfing is therapeutic for the participants. Plus, I'd learned more about autism than I could have ever imagined.

So, that morning in the hotel lobby in Jacksonville, my goodbyes to the SFA family were far more than a hug and a promise to call soon.

It was the closing chapter in my story of surfing and autism.

In the months and years to come, I kept track of every family I'd spent time with, seeing heartwarming change from thousands of miles away.

For the Fuentes family, there has been significant change since the 2015 SFA season. In 2016, after 8 years of service with SFA, the family took a hiatus. They returned to the organization in 2019, with Alfie Fuentes taking on the role of Director of Operations and Laura working as the Administrative Director.

"Our family benefited immensely from SFA over the years and I am happy that we will once again be able to have a positive impact on the autism community," Alfie said.

"SFA has been life-changing for us," Laura added. "It has given our family the ability to know what it's like to be accepting, kind, brave and understanding. We have made lifelong friends and Lucas found a place in the world."

In recent years, Miranda became an EMT and a member of the Fire Academy. Her plan is to follow in Alfie's footsteps and be a firefighter, working in environments—similar to SFA—where she can help others. Alfie became a Captain for the Hollywood Fire Department in South Florida. Lucas was accepted to the renowned Els Center of Excellence, a school for autism. Lucas "has made some big strides academically and socially," according to Laura. Besides his love for the beach and surfing, he has a new love for painting and golf, and he continues to enjoy movies. Youngest brother Oliver graduated middle school, entered high school and is currently in an International Baccalaureate program.

Even with these changes, a few things have stayed the same, like the important bond between the siblings. "Miranda and Oliver take incredible care of Lucas; all three enjoy taking trips together and love spending time together," Laura said. Their love for the ocean is a mainstay as well: if the family takes a vacation, sand and waves are priorities on the itinerary. Visit an SFA event or other autism awareness events around the South Florida and Treasure Coast area, and you'll likely see the family.

Outside of school and other activities, the Weppner family has spent as much time as possible at Nate's happy place—the beach—attending SFA events and making friends at their local beach.

It's those friends that have seen the most progress in Nate, according to Michele.

"They say he's calmer, more engaged," she says. "Me too; I've seen a big difference in him. He's saying things, sleeping better, getting stronger. It's a constant work in progress."

The "big difference" Michele has seen is certainly attributable in part to the surfing and community aspects of SFA. The surfing organization hasn't just helped Nate, though.

"It's helped us as a family," Michele said. "Especially for my oldest son Daniel, to see other families coping and going through similar issues, and that we're not the only ones experiencing it. I'm so grateful and blessed SFA came into my life."

Looking forward, the family is excited to take Nate surfing in upcoming events. And whether it's at the beach or elsewhere, Michele and the Weppner family will forever be advocating for Nate, helping him progress, and celebrating every accomplishment along the way.

Since I last saw Damian, he has grown taller, further refined his surfing skill, and entered high school. He is completely mainstreamed and does not have a shadow or an aide. In his freshman year, which Tracy Basante said went "excellent" overall, he maintained A's and B's in his classes and joined the drama club, taking part in a school musical.

Damian's appetite for surfing competition has only increased with time. He qualified for the State Surfing Championships for Special Olympics in 2016, 2017 and 2018. In 2016, utilizing the skills he learned at SFA events, he won the silver medal in his division.

He continues to surf at SFA events and compete in local surf competitions. He also joined the Eastern Surf Association, a historic contest organization that has fanned the competitive flame for some of the East Coast's best surfers, including two male surfers who became world champions.

While many Damian's age are still searching for their passions, Damian already has his, along with an identity and a community of friends and family.

Like Tracy and Damian, the Arnold family has continued to attend SFA events, and has incorporated other activities to quench Christopher's adventurous spirit, including karate and CrossFit. As Christopher nears graduation from high school—where he chose to have a surfboard inscribed on his senior class ring—he has continued to improve academically, and according to Linda, he's been "trying so hard to talk."

Keith admits there have been several "small victories" recently, which are especially evident on SFA event days. After catching the waves, Christopher now volunteers, helping with miscellaneous tasks, like deconstructing the event tents in the afternoon. He also gets visibly excited watching other participants catch waves and experience breakthroughs. As Keith puts it, "He wants everyone to be happy and to be included."

These "small victories" extend outside of surfing, too: Christopher's church Confirmation went well, and he attended the Tim Tebow Foundation Night to Shine, which acts as a prom, multiple times with different dates. His reading level has increased, and he continues to work with a device that helps him communicate. The family still embarks on thrilling vacations, which include activities like hiking for over a mile, and skiing. In fact, Christopher, with the help of an instructor, recently skied through the middle of an Olympic halfpipe, completely enamored with the high icy walls that surrounded him.

Because the best indicator of future behavior is past behavior, it's safe to say that the Arnold's future will be filled with more of the same: focusing on Christopher's developmental growth and outdoor adventures—including surfing—along the way.

After eleven years, over 100 events, and thousands of participants, Don and Kim Ryan are passing the torch of Surfers For Autism to someone new. They are looking forward to starting a new journey.

Surfing continues to be an integral part of life for the Poe family. Evan now has his own surfboard and has developed a passion for paddle-boarding. Ethan has shown a desire to improve his surfing ability. "Ethan watches other surfers—he's analyzing and mimicking how they do it, processing in the now," Bob said.

Socially, Evan continues to make friends on the beach and Ethan has been coming out of his shell more and more. According to Christine, "Ethan often has his nose in his phone, he doesn't want to give it up. But during event days, he doesn't even touch his phone." Older sister Abbey, undoubtedly impacted by her brother's challenges, is pursuing a college degree in American Sign Language.

The family has also created a company, birthed from their passion for water sports, the desire to create work experience for Ethan and Evan as they grow older, and the realization of just how hard it can be for young adults with autism to get a job.

The story goes that one afternoon, while Bob was paddle-boarding with Evan, Evan said the words "electric fish." Bob, mishearing him, thought he said "eclectic fish", and replied, "That's what you are. You're my eclectic fish." Thus, Eclectic Fish Water Company was born, manufacturing surfing, SUP, and longboard accessories. The family not only wants to provide work experience for their children—they want to provide jobs for others with special needs as well.

When Bob thinks about how far their family has come, from him and Christine meeting, to marriage, having kids, the autism diagnosis, surfing, and starting a company, he says, "Autism has changed our life for the better."

Not only has Skye continued surfing at SFA events; she also volunteers with other participants, helping to spread the excitement she feels while surfing. According to Kami, "She wants to give back to the people who have given her so much."

Outside of SFA, Skye has been participating in Special Olympics surfing for the past three years. In 2018, she yet again competed in the State Championships. Although she aimed for gold, she enjoys the fun of surfing, not so much the competition.

Now that she can catch her own waves — in 2019 she'll turn 19 — she has been working further on her tricks on her longboard. According to Kami, she's "Trying to get the crossover walking to the nose of the board."

Skye has also realized the therapeutic benefits of surfing herself. "She made up new words to the Twenty-One Pilots song "Blurry Face," singing that she loves to surf when she's stressed out," Kami said. "She has told me often how surfing calms her and is a stress reducer."

Skye will graduate high school in May of 2019, and wants to pursue college education. "In her college admission essay, she wrote that she wants to bring Autism Awareness to people, that just because someone has autism, they shouldn't be stereotyped and it shouldn't keep them from being able to do what they want to do," Kami said. Other than college, Skye wants to travel abroad as well, someplace where she can, of course, surf.

In 2015, while riding in the car with Abigail, Asa, and Priscilla to Abigail's school, I noticed Asa creating a video to show Abigail's teachers the progress she had made with the task of brushing her teeth. In the years since I had seen the family, Asa had used his video knowledge and his quick-learning skill-set to set up a YouTube vlog called "Fathering Autism." The vlog, which reached over 100,000 followers in 2018, chronicles the family's efforts to battle the stigma of autism, and provides a firsthand look at the struggles, joy, and comedy of what it's like to truly father autism.

These episodes are as fascinating to watch as any award-winning television program. Covering topics like potty training, meltdowns in Wal-Mart, haircuts, road trips, learning to speak at 13, and more, the videos provide a glimpse into Abigail's life—and most importantly, they offer valuable insight into autism along the way. The family even won a Shorty Award, which honors the "best of social media by recognizing the influencers, brands, and organizations."

The family has also decided to help out the cause internationally. After hearing from a SFA volunteer about a boy living with nonverbal autism in a remote village in El Salvador, they raised money for supplies to aid his needs. Isaiah and another SFA volunteer made the trek to personally deliver these supplies, venturing up a mountain to hand the boy a walker and forearm crutches. The boy, who had been abandoned by his mother and was living with his grandmother in a village that relies on farming and fishing to survive, could suddenly walk and move freely for the first time in his life. This was certainly a profoundly emotional experience for Isaiah, now a high school student; he hopes to plan a return trip in the near future.

Besides attending SFA events so that Abigail can continue her progress with surfing, she has also been working towards more independence at home, such as by prepping meals, folding clothes, cleaning tables, and other household chores. She also continues to improve her communication skills using an alternative communication device, according to Priscilla.

From the sands of SFA events to the mountains of El Salvador and the homepage of their YouTube vlog, the Maass' will continue to be advocates for autism awareness.

While each of these families has seen change in some form, there are some things that will not change, even as time continues to speed by, namely the memories, the progress, and the lessons learned during those salty, sunny, and sandy days on the beach; and, most importantly, the hope. The hope that every parent and volunteer has on every event day: that surfing will help either their child or someone else in need.

It's that hope that will reverberate from this day to the next, forever in search of pieces to complete the autism puzzle.

ACKNOWLEDGEMENTS

There were many people who had an integral part in the creation of this book, from those who played a part in my journalism education to those who helped me edit the book's pages.

First and foremost, I want to thank my Lord and Savior Jesus Christ. Without Him being such a powerful force in my life, none of this—from my blessed life to this book—would have been possible.

I am forever indebted to the Surfers for Autism community. To Don and Kim Ryan, thank you for your incredible, life-changing work with Surfers for Autism and for allowing me to tell these stories of breakthroughs. I'm grateful for your unyielding encouragement throughout the process.

To each of the families involved in this book: the Fuentes, the Poes, Kami and Skye, Tracy and Damian, Byron, the Maass', the Arnolds, the Weppners and more: thank you for inviting me into your homes, into your lives, and trusting me with your personal tales. Each of you became my friends throughout the process. You made me laugh, you made me cry, and most importantly, you inspired me. Truthfully, the best memories I have from my time with all of you is not when I was interviewing you for the book; rather, it was when you made me feel like family. When you invited me to sit at your dinner table, spend time with you at event afterparties, and watch your emotional, raw reactions as you proudly watched your children surf. Thank you.

There were many other SFA family members who had an impact on me in this process, helping me to understand the intricacies of autism and offering me friendship. Thank you.

To my family: I owe a big thank you to my parents, Steve and Tammy, and my brother Chase. You all entertained so many conversations with me about this book, either on the phone, at the dinner table, while walking the Las Vegas Strip, or while hiking Kauai's rugged NaPali Coast. Dad, thank you for encouraging me throughout this process, and for giving me tips and ideas along the way, all of which made this book better. Mom, thank you for your unconditional and motivating support. I love you both.

To my grandparents: Bill and Vera Downs. Both of you have had a lifelong impact on me as a person and as a writer. Bill, thank you for introducing me to the intricacies of journalism at such a young and formative age. Your articles, your two fascinating books, and the quality of the relationships you had with your journalism students made a lifelong impact on me. Vera, thank you for your unconditional love and for editing the pages of this book—there's no doubt that it reads better thanks to you.

There are many editors in the outdoor industry who deserve a thank you for giving me a chance to work alongside them throughout my maturation, which ultimately led to this book. To Steve Bowman, thank you for taking me under your wing at *ESPN Outdoors* and *The Outdoor Channel,* and for entrusting me with editorial assignments on a local and national scale. I cherish the conversations we had in your office, filled with books, magazines, camera lenses, and press credentials. You taught me not only how to be a better writer, but how to be a better man. Thank you.

To Nick McGregor and the *Eastern Surf Magazine* family: thank you for granting me my very first byline in the surf media so many years ago—it was something that was not given easily. And thank you for entertaining my constant story idea pitches, allowing me to contribute to your publication.

To Taylor Paul, Beau Flemister, and the *Surfing Magazine* staff: thank you for entrusting me with an international editorial assignment, and for allowing me to contribute to a media outlet I've revered for years.

To my closest friends: Ben, Ethan, Brandon, and Josh, thank you for your continual support throughout the creation of this book.

To Palm Beach Atlantic University: I'm grateful for your "workship" volunteer program, which was the initial reason why I attended an SFA event. The program, and the University as a whole, showed me the importance of having a volunteer mindset and what amazing things can come to fruition because of it. This book is certainly an example.

To Hatherleigh Press: Ryan Kennedy, Ryan Tumambing, and Andrew Flach, thank you for your incredible efforts, from believing in this book to editing its pages and bringing this book to publication.

Last but certainly not least: thank you to everyone who reads this book. My hope is that the stories that fill these pages have the same impact on you that they had on me, and that they inspire you to lend a helping hand in some way.

ABOUT THE AUTHOR

Cash Lambert is a former Editor for Hawaii's *Freesurf Magazine.* He currently lives on Oahu's North Shore. His articles have been featured in *ESPN Outdoors, Surfing Magazine, Eastern Surf Magazine,* the *Outdoor Channel, Surfline, Stab Magazine, Autism Parenting Magazine, The Atlantic Current, Flux* and more. While pursuing his undergraduate degree at Palm Beach Atlantic University, Cash was awarded with the Bodie McDowell Scholarship from the Outdoor Writers Association of America for his editorial work. A graduate from PBA's School of Communication and Media, he majored in Journalism. He served as a volunteer and surf instructor with Surfers for Autism for four years.

BIBLIOGRAPHY

Chapter 2
1. www.cdc.gov/ncbddd/Autism/facts.html
2. www.cdc.gov/ncbddd/Autism/facts.html
3. www.Autismspeaks.org/what-Autism/symptoms
4. www.cdc.gov/ncbddd/Autism/data.html
5. www.Autismspeaks.org/what-Autism/prevalence
6. www.Autism-society.org/what-is/facts-and-statistics/

Chapter 7
1. Nichols, Wallace J. Blue Mind: The Surprising Science That Shows How Being Near, In, On, or Under Water Can Make You Happier, Healthier, More Connected, and Better at What You Do. 115-16.
2. Nichols, Wallace J. Blue Mind: The Surprising Science That Shows How Being Near, In, On, or Under Water Can Make You Happier, Healthier, More Connected, and Better at What You Do. 175.
3. Nichols, Wallace J. Blue Mind: The Surprising Science That Shows How Being Near, In, On, or Under Water Can Make You Happier, Healthier, More Connected, and Better at What You Do. 174-175.

Chapter 11
1. www.Autismspeaks.org/what-Autism/facts-about-Autism